HANDS-ON
LOG HOMES

HANDS-ON
LOG HOMES

CINDY & ART THIEDE

PHOTOGRAPHY BY JEFF WALLING AND CINDY THIEDE

GIBBS·SMITH
P
PUBLISHER

SALT LAKE CITY

First edition
01 00 99 98 5 4 3 2 1

Published by Gibbs Smith, Publisher
P.O. Box 667
Layton, Utah 84041
TO ORDER BOOKS: (1-800) 748-5439
VISIT OUR WEB SITE: WWW.GIBBS-SMITH.COM

Printed and bound in Hong Kong
Design by Leesha Jones, Moon and Stars Design

Front jacket photograph: Randell and Trisha Mayer home
Back jacket photograph: Steve and Celia Abbey living room

LIBRARY OF CONGRESS CATALOGING-IN-PUBLICATION DATA
Thiede, Cindy Teipner, 1958–
Hands-on log homes / Cindy Thiede and Art Thiede ; photography by Jeff Walling and Cindy Thiede. — 1st ed.
p.   cm.
Includes bibliographical references.
ISBN 0-87905-805-6
1. Log cabins—United States—Design and construction—Popular works. 2. Log cabins—United States—Conservation and restoration—Popular works. I. Thiede, Arthur. II. Title.
TH4840.T45   1998
690'.873—dc21   98-14031
                                            CIP

Dedicated to Stanley Thiede

We had never heard of Stanley Thiede before the fall of 1996. Since he and Art both trace their roots back to northern Germany, we suppose they might actually be related. But that isn't why we want to dedicate this book to him.

At nearly eighty years of age, Stanley is a holdout. Of course, he lives in a log cabin. It was built around 1875. Stanley's parents bought it more than ninety years ago, and he grew up there along with his brother and sister. In time, Stanley's parents passed on, and his siblings moved away in pursuit of families and opportunities more suited to the times.

Not Stanley. Never married, he stayed on to care for the old homestead, and he's still there today. Not much has changed—at least not on his property. The house has never had plumbing or electricity—just a one-hole privy out back. Stanley still lowers a bucket into a well that was hand dug more than 120 years ago. He wrangles up biscuits and stew on the cast-iron stove that

came with the place when his parents bought it. Oh, the floors sag here and there; and sure, the stairs tilt and creak just a bit, but Stanley's cabin bears the comfortable marks of family, the curious marks of history, the indelible marks of home.

Stanley has held onto a way of life that few would or could. Some might say he's missed out, but Stanley doesn't see it that way. He's got Mike, his dog. He's got friends, and he's got stories—plenty of them. As for all those "mansions" on the hills around him—well, Stanley will tell you right out that "they're kind of an eyesore."

Then the corners of his mouth will curl up under his bushy mustache and he'll stand a little taller as he explains how special his simple home is. It's official. After more than a year of hard work, the Thiede cabin in Golden, Colorado, is listed on the National Register of Historic Places—and that, says Stanley, "is good enough for me!"

CONTENTS

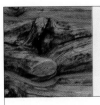

Acknowledgments

A book like ours is only possible when a whole lot of people open their doors and say "come on in," then sit back and reminisce while we rearrange their furniture. For us, traveling from state to state and log home to log home was nothing less than a marvelous odyssey into the lives of extraordinary, ordinary families. For all those warm welcomes, engaging visits, and charitable meals, Jeff Walling and I are very grateful. Apart from that, I want to extend a sincere thank you to the countless number of individuals who served as inspiration for this book. We received piles of mail in response to our advertisements for owner-involved log homes. So many people wrote passionate accounts of their own building adventures that we couldn't begin to visit or include them all here. We did, however, laugh, groan, marvel with, and celebrate each one's accomplishments as we read their letters and shared their pictures.

To my friends Patti, Patrice, Karol, Lisa, Heather, Doots, and Lise Mousel-Martini, thanks for all the support and little extras during that seemingly endless gestation of book birthing. And to those high-spirited boys in my life—Art, Tyler and Jesse—a whole jar full of marbles for enduring my "on the road" months as a family of three. Finally, thanks to our editor, Madge Baird, for her professional, no-nonsense approach to getting the job done right!

ABOVE Personalized tools of the trade and a pair of triumphant boots mark the rights of passage for their exuberant owner, Bob Fulton. He began his hewn log home a novice but finished it a craftsman.

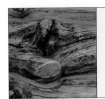

PREFACE

This book, our third on log homes, is part of that elusive thing called destiny, and it all started at a truck and car show in the summer of 1990. That was the day my husband, Art, stumbled across a green 1936 flatbed Chevy truck. It was for sale but had a price tag that wasn't in our budget (I say "ours" because, had I been home with the flu that day, the truck most likely would have been in Art's budget). The day passed, and I went on about my business as if I had never seen that truck in my life. In fact, years passed.

We built our own log home, lived in it, loved it, then sold it so we could do it all over again. Our new house was built to resemble an old farmhouse, with squared gray logs and posted corners. We uprooted the restored windmill planted in the pasture of our former home and moved it to our new spread. Next came a red, two-story log barn with white trim, a gambrel roof, and a hundred-year-old school bell in the cupola. Antique farm equipment and old signs dressed the barn walls and surrounding yard. The only things missing were the chickens, goats, and—you guessed it—a green truck.

Actually, the first time I noticed that the green truck was "missing" was the day Art asked me how I'd feel if he bought himself a little Christmas present. "Sure, why not. What do you want?"

"Well . . . , I really need a green truck." he said. As it turns out, he had already bought it. Now, that may surprise you—though it didn't me. The surprise was that he had bought it a whole year earlier. It was stowed in its former owner's yard, but with a heavy winter coming on, the time had come to move it to its rightful home.

That is how the truck came to live in our barn. But that isn't the whole story, because once the truck was in the barn, Art had to do something with it. That something was to restore it. Then, of course, something had to be done with the restored truck (now we're getting closer to the origins of this book).

As it happens, through all those years, that truck had spoken to Art's soul. It begged him back to another place and time. Now, inspired anew, it had become very clear to him that what we needed to do was simplify— that is, sell our house along with *everything* else we owned, except the kids. The plan was to buy moviemaking gear, load the family into the old truck (kids in back), and head out across the Midwest to make a film documentary for public television on the American water-pumping windmill. While we were at it, we would do a book, too (on windmills, not log homes). Had things gone according to plan, we would have entered the truck in our local Fourth of July parade, then just kept on going into the sunrise (a sort of *Grapes of Wrath* in reverse, observed one amused friend).

Well, it didn't happen that way at all. A movie proposition was too spendy, funding too hard to come by, and the honest truth is I wasn't completely sold on the concept. We did run the windmill book idea past our publisher, who was mildly interested but suggested that a book on small log homes might work better for him. Now, I'm not saying that someday you won't read about us stirring up dust in Kansas, visiting truck-parts stores and repair shops, and photographing windmills (undoubtedly, in that order). Maybe you will—but not yet.

It seems that our lives move in circles. As a couple, Art and I started out in an aging Dodge van. Nearly everything we owned fit under the makeshift bed in back. We eventually moved into a rented condominium, then Art started building with logs. Our goal was to own a log home of our own, and we have since built three for ourselves. Our current home is my favorite, and you will read about it in this book. Nevertheless, we will soon pass this home on to a new family who shares a little something of the dream and vision from which it was created. Where to next? Are we ready to chuck it all for life in the back of a '36 Chevy flatbed? I don't know. We do, however, seem to be following a path around the circle of our own lives and returning, if not literally then at least philosophically, towards a less cluttered, less complicated lifestyle. For us, this book on not-so-big, owner-built log homes comes at a time when our hearts are in the same place as our heads.

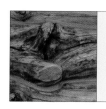

INTRODUCTION

We wanted pictures and floor plans of small log homes built and designed at least in part by their owners, and our ads said so. We'd managed to put the word out in nearly half a dozen building publications around the country. When the mail started pouring in, Art and I were too anxious to read the letters, so they got tossed to the side while we raced through piles of point-and-click pictures sent by anonymous owners. A few of the snapshots were good. Some were okay, but others were . . . well, er . . . snapshots! You know how it is—some were dark, others were fuzzy, and some were dark and fuzzy! At the bottom of the stack, we'd often sit back and wonder what exactly we were looking for. We wanted small homes, or at least not big ones. Mostly we were looking for owners who were on a budget. We wanted them to be involved in homes that were doable and yet a little out of the ordinary. As it turned out, we were so busy looking for diamonds that we completely missed the pearls.

It wasn't until I had gone back and carefully read each letter that those fuzzy, too-dark, too-light pictures came into focus. Maybe those homeowners weren't all photographers, but they were people of real vision with extraordinary stories of determination and purpose. Most of them had regular jobs and regular incomes, but I wouldn't call any of them average. For many, a hand-crafted log home would not have been financially possible without the generous infusion of their own sweat equity. For others, taking on a house-building project with logs was the opportunity to challenge their own resourcefulness, vent powerful creative energy, and say loud and clear, "Yes, I can!"

That log homes are something different today from what they were a few decades back is obvious. Of course they're bigger. In the past ten years the average living space in a cabin has more than doubled to nearly 2,300 square feet, and custom handcrafted homes are typically *much* larger. They have shed their rustic backwoods image, and nine out of ten are individualized for owners who consider them their primary residence. Log homes generally cost 10 to 30 percent more to build than their conventionally framed counterparts. Architects, artisans, and designers take log homes seriously and have decked them out, imbued them with sophistication, and set them up as the eighth wonder of the architectural world. Indeed, they are wonderful, but all this fuss and attention has carried the industry to a place where many cannot follow. In the process of growing up, the cabins of yesterday's dreams now sit on foundations that far fewer can afford.

Having tracked the course of log building in the United States for more than fifteen years, Art and I don't excuse our own involvement in this spiraling log-home trend. Through our books *American Log Homes* and *The Log Home Book*, we sought to capture the excitement that surrounded the industry as log homes recycled back into the consciousness of mainstream American homeowners after their long though not forgotten exile on syrup labels, toy cartons, and history pages. Reveling in the amazing possibilities of logs in home architecture, we leaned towards the most spectacular megahomes we could find. Now, several years later, as we stop to glance back and catch our breath, we feel a small twinge of regret—not for what we have embraced but for what and who we have left out.

After all, small family-initiated cabins first drew the dreamer in, and many of the romantic notions we cling to are reminiscent of those humble beginnings. Today a contingent of dedicated do-it-yourselfers is still quietly at work in America. Unlike our forebears, they are not building with logs because they have to but because they want to, because they can, and sometimes because they believe it's the right thing to do. Although the trend in our country has been towards big, bigger, and biggest, it's the niches and nooks that people are drawn to. Everybody talks about "intimate spaces," but they're hard to find in cavernous great rooms, restaurant-sized kitchens, and commodious master suites.

What is small? Within our own privileged borders we define that differently depending on where we live, the size of our families, our lifestyle, relative affluence, and the purpose for which we design our homes. Yet within that broad framework one thing remains: the decision to build small (or *smaller*) is as much an attitude as it is a conscious choice. Whether born of necessity or desire, building a successful home of modest size and proportion is more challenging than building a large house because you can't solve your design problems by merely adding square feet.

As a building medium, logs are not chosen lightly, but if they are your heart's desire, then you are a kindred spirit with many of the homeowners in this book. These are the pictures and stories of people who have put mod-

est foundations under big dreams. Many of them did much of the work themselves, saving many dollars along the way. For fun we have tried to list approximate house-building costs for different projects but caution you that owner-builders working cash-out-of-pocket over a period of years are notoriously bad bookkeepers. It is also important to realize that, apart from being out-of-date, one estimate might include such things as a well, septic system, and site prep, while another may simply calculate the costs of building materials. In other words, don't take these numbers to the bank or to your local log-home producer!

This is by no means a how-to-build book, but along with true-grit tales of ceaseless dedication, we offer a little direction, some commonsense advice, and a bunch of dreamable ideas. Not every house is entirely owner built. Skilled craftsmen were sometimes called upon to anchor fancy in reality. This is particularly true in the chapter "Handmade Originals," on historical restorations. Yet, as lovers of logs, we include these paternal treasures because they remain our link to the past.

No matter what level of sophistication logs ultimately take on in contemporary architecture, there remains something pure and uncomplicated about them—something so endearing to those of us who work the wood or cry out for less-chaotic lifestyles. Of course, this is partly fantasy, but that's what we like about them, too. Regardless of how we're led, there is beauty in "small" and tremendous satisfaction in a home that stands even in part by the work of our own hands.

1 BACK TO BASICS

RIGHT The ghosts of yesteryear may yet linger in the cottage garden outside this 16-by-20-foot cabin believed to have been built around 1770. Restored by Charles McRaven as a studio for quilting author Jinny Byer, little cabins like this one were often home to exceptionally large families.

I grew up in a grand white house with a long-winded baritone doorbell. When I was ten, I bet my parents ten dollars that I could feed myself for a week on five bucks. Though I possibly bought enough peanut butter and jelly to last, I don't remember making it past dinner that night! In college I shared an itty-bitty house with three other roommates. We furnished the entire place with cinder blocks, plywood, and free beer mugs from the local hip-hop joint. My room and board didn't amount to much more than $100 per month (though I think my entertainment budget probably rivaled that). When I met my husband, Art, he lived in a one-room cabin and paid even less than I did. When he came for a week-long visit, he brought everything he thought he might need (including his boots) in a day-pack that wouldn't hold the books I carried to three classes.

In my growing years, I took my homes for granted, not understanding nor particularly caring how much they influenced my life and, likewise, how much they revealed about me. (Oh, I got an inkling when I visited Art, and realized how much his home revealed about him!) Of course, I know now that a real home is much more than a roof over your head. As a child, *home* was my four-poster bed, the Early American antiques collected by my mother, and a home-cooked meatloaf dinner that, try as I may, I could not pass up for ten bucks or peanut butter and jelly. Home was security.

The one-room cabin of Art's early adulthood was mostly a function of his lifestyle and a reflection of the things he valued—few of which were material. Later when he and I joined together to design and build our own first log house it was a time to test and nurture our relationship and build confidence in our abilities. Home was a proving ground for cooperative living and the beginning of our family life together.

Two sons came along in time, and our home today continues to be a nearly indescribable jumble of those familiar and personal things that matter most—intensified all the more by the fact that we built it ourselves. The physical and mental investment that goes into the building process links a family to their home in ways that a market-bought house never could. It's hugely rewarding! Apart from that, home ownership is in itself an "American Dream" come true. For many home owners, that dream must be financed in part through their own time and labor. Acting as your own general contractor can save you from 10 to 25 percent of the total value of the home without so much as lifting a log—or quitting your regular job.

That amount can be doubled or tripled, depending on how much of the work you are willing or able to do yourself—provided you can reconcile the fact that your time has value too.

A few greenhorns will tackle an entire log-house project single-handedly. Others will take on a significant amount of the work, hiring out only a handful of jobs that require skills they cannot master or that must be subcontracted out to comply with local building codes. Still

BELOW This tiny mining shack hints at the solitary rugged life of Leadking Paul and his canine companion, Boy Dog. Immersed in another place and time, the pair must don packs, then ski, hike, or snowshoe seven miles through the Colorado Rockies to pick up a T-bone or a can of beans.

ABOVE Covered porches
shield log walls from the
elements while adding
protected space for dining,
relaxation, and storage.
Because porches cut down on
sunlight, the Mayers
incorporated skylights over
their decks.

others will act as their own designer,
project manager, or job-site grunt. How
much you can do will depend on your
energy level, willingness to learn, and the
size of your commitment. It will also hinge
on the scale and complexity of the house
you intend to build. If you're on fire but
untried, a small workable design will keep
you on target.

The Case for Small

America today is not so much a do-
it-yourself society, but we were once. The
pioneers were successful in part because
those early cabins were small and their
designs were simple affairs. Although they

didn't have two cars, three TVs and an RV,
chances are those first families did have
eight or ten kids. Times have changed, and
a successful design must accommodate our
present-day lifestyle. On the other hand,
we are not really conditioned to thinking
honestly about our needs—nor are we
motivated simply by what works. Our ten-
dency is to turn our homes into status sym-
bols, and while they may inadvertently
become that, to make it the driving force
behind a design can be costly, wasteful,
and ultimately disappointing.

Maintaining an attitude towards
small and doable may mean making due
without some of the pomp and show, de-
voting yourself to a simpler lifestyle, or

owning less junk. Whatever the trade-offs, consider the rewards. From the very beginning, such a house requires fewer resources to build—starting with the logs themselves. As responsible builders, we should know that the same whole trees we stack so lovingly in our walls will satisfy the lumber needs of two or more similar-sized frame houses. We often choose logs because they prickle our earthly senses, and in an age of ever-diminishing natural resources, using less may simply be the right thing to do.

That we save money by using less and doing less is obvious. Not only is the wood expensive, but log homes are notoriously labor-intensive to build and finish. Curvy walls meet in bumpy corners. Nothing is quite square, and there's a good deal more scribing, carving, and cajoling that comes with the territory. Hired out, the doing part is always costly, but time itself is the owner-builder's most precious commodity.

A well-built small home will save in other ways, too. It will be more ecological in its energy requirements, thus less expensive to heat and cool. Fewer square feet equate to lower annual property taxes. A small home may also enable you to spend more cash out-of-pocket and reduce or eliminate your reliance on a bank loan. Maintenance becomes less spendy and cumbersome too. Preserving the

BELOW Randell and Trisha Mayers built an 800-square-foot cottage, then added oodles of seasonal living space with wraparound porches.

natural glow of just-peeled logs may require special attention every few years. Build any home—especially a large one—without anticipating the upkeep (and cleaning), and you may well sabotage the enjoyment of more than just your extra spending cash and future weekends.

Whatever spiritual or worldly motivator sets our hearts towards logs, we can be sure that there will be difficult design choices ahead. Even the most disciplined among us will rise in battle with our budget. Just the prospect of designing your own home sets the right brain cranking. Any longed-for amenities, extravagant or not, beg remembrance. A home-warming stone hearth, handcrafted spiral stairway, round-top picture windows, built-in bays, or vaulted ceilings might present themselves as must-have features. This is a good time to keep in mind that the design process is just that—a process. Examining and sorting through your wants may help you clarify your commitment to a small home or perhaps even your commitment to logs. Some things will have to go, and there will be trade-offs. In the end, perhaps you will sacrifice overall size for expensive extras that would otherwise be impractical. In this case, "quality over quantity" may become your credo.

First Things First

There are hundreds of considerations to contemplate when you embark down the building path, and a natural progression of events to help you get to the end. The centerpiece of a triumphant home is a successful plan, but the starting place is with your finances. First you must decide how much you have to spend, then you must decide how much you *really* have to spend. Whether you will be taking out a loan or working with cash out-of-pocket, you should have a realistic upper limit. If you will be stretching out your home-building project over a period of years, you'll still want to plan in phases and budget accordingly.

As with any house, the dollars spent on the building itself are only a portion of the whole enchilada. Before your first log is laid, you will have to purchase land and prepare your site. You may need a road, and if you aren't in proximity to existing sewer and water, you will need a septic system, well, or water-collection device. There may also be associated state or local fees to pay. These costs can gobble up a significant portion of your anticipated budget if you haven't done your homework and planned accordingly.

With those primary concerns at least on the list, you can turn your attention to the house. The options to consider begin with the wood itself. Will you harvest trees on your own land, buy them raw from a broker, or purchase a log shell in some varying state of readiness? It is estimated that around 25,000 log homes get built each year in the United States. Of those, most will start out as packages prepared by companies galore offering a boggling array of log wall and corner styles. At the root of this prolific family tree, companies classify themselves in one of two ways: those that offer machine-milled or manufactured homes and those that distinguish themselves as being handcrafters.

The milled-log-home producer utilizes modern machinery to mass-produce piles of same-sized, precision-peeled, and notched logs. Homes built with these systems are generally more affordable because a whole lot less elbow grease goes into their construction and assembly. Likewise, companies can and commonly do utilize smaller, less-expensive logs. Manufacturers pride themselves on the ability to offer a great diversity of styles—ranging from those considered traditional to many others that incorporate intricate tongue-and-groove joinery between each course of logs.

Regardless of the style, machine-carved logs present a home more finished in appearance and less akin to its rustic predecessors—a fact that is sometimes disappointing to a would-be buyer. Yet, because many consumers must be painfully value-conscious to attain log-home ownership at all, they may select a milled-log package over a handcrafted one in compromise. In defense, companies sensitive to their clients' wishes are coming up with new ways to blur the line between themselves and their handcrafted competitors. Some will now rough up their machine-peeled logs with drawknives or adzes for a hand-peeled look.

Manufactured log homes are generally sold in packages or kits that come in varying degrees of completeness and price. Unlike the handcrafted counterpart, exacting machinery creates building components that usually do not need to be preassembled before shipping. With the help of efficient high-tech equipment, a single miller can provide a hundred or more families with log shells each year.

A handcrafted log home is still keyed to the basic tenet of muscle and a wet brow. Each trunk is peeled by hand, then every log, post, and beam is carefully measured and shaped to fit in its place. While some artisans prefer to craft their homes entirely on-site, most companies will pre-build the log shells in their own work yards. The logs in each home are then numbered and the building disassembled for shipment to the owner's land, where it will be reerected. Because handcrafted log homes are so labor intensive, most companies manage to produce only four to eight shells per year. There are exceptions, and a few bigger companies will put out considerably more homes. Even so, the demand is often greater than the industry's ability to meet, so there can be a substantial waiting period before any given company can take on a new project.

Though only a rough generalization, any company-produced log shell will consume a quarter to a third of the total house budget when built by the usual contingent of paid labor. Do some or all of the remaining work yourself, and you can write your own receipt. For you hearty souls who harvest your own trees, the cost savings and satisfaction of building from scratch may climb exponentially *if* you are competent in the woods, have the time to season your logs, and can muster the notching and joinery skills dictated by your project.

The Centerpiece of Success

Whether you go with a log-home company or tackle the job yourself, your home design is the seed from which your project flourishes or flounders. It is at this stage of conception that you nurture or cull the many elements that will combine to make this building your home. It is not unusual for families to spend two, three, or more years gathering, sorting, and processing the information that goes into their final plan.

There are several places to poke around, including the obvious books and magazines, some of which are listed in our

ABOVE As the regional sales manager for Hearthstone Log Homes, Jon Lauderdale enjoyed special savings when completing his own home from a company-built shell. These rough-sawn logs were hand notched, then machine hewn and sandblasted.

resource section. Of course, these printed sources have no shortage of drop-dead, gorgeous, kabillion-dollar homes. Clip out those great ideas, but beware: when you approach the design process pumped up by such commanding images, you risk cardiac arrest when figuring your costs!

Get a feel for what's possible, then research some more to find out what's doable. Talk to company representatives and check out their model homes. If you plan to work from a kit or hire a handcrafter, ask for references. Talk with and visit former clients to see the finished product

and get the inside scoop. Attend log-home shows, seminars, and workshops. Then, if you will be doing all or most of the work yourself, take time out to enroll in a hands-on log-building clinic. While people can and do learn technique out of books, you will probably master skills faster and make fewer errors having worked by the side of an expert.

Where Does All That Money Go?

A small, value-conscious log house adheres to some basic building principles. These are the beginning places. Start with the minimum to meet your personal and aesthetic needs, then enlarge or embellish as your budget and talents allow.

• Notching and joinery add the touch of Midas in a well-crafted log home. Jogs in the wall, interior corners, snazzy bays, and the like draw praise, but they come with a price. Each zig and zag demand extra time and skilled labor, so the closer you come to a rectangle with four corners, the easier and less expensive your home will be to build. Adversely, the more intricate your building footprint, the more complicated your foundation and roof become, along with nearly everything else in between.

• To paraphrase a well-known building axiom, it is more economical to build up or down than it is to build out. A roof is often the single most expensive component on a structure, so if you can add square footage without incurring additional roofing costs, you will save money. The addition of a second story instead of a second wing will save on heating and foundation work too. In the case of a base-

BELOW A woodstove is not only a cost-effective alternative to a full masonry fireplace but a pleasant and economical way to heat a home. It is especially practical in open homes like Bob and France Kudelski's, where nearly every room in the house is visible from the living-room couch.

LEFT Not overly concerned with privacy, the Kudelskis' master bedroom is partially open to the living space below. A large shed dormer was added to create walk-around space in their gable-end room. Custom Log Homes provided the log package.

ment, you will need a deeper hole and more concrete, but the extra dollars spent on excavation and foundation work are usually less than the expense of more roof.

• Basements are always worth exploring in a budget-conscious design, but natural light will make them truly livable. If you find yourself with a workable sloping site, consider the ideal—a walk-out or daylight basement. Where good soil, proper drainage, and accessibility line up with pleasant view and sun corridors, you could have all the ingredients you need to take advantage of this economical building option.

• There is no question that unusual rooflines create elevations that are visually exciting. Coupled with magnificent log or timber trusses, full-log gable ends, and vaulted ceilings inside, you have a home that is as expensive as it is grand. You can hold onto more of your money, again, by simplifying your design and by building a conventionally framed roof, then adding non-structural logs and timbers for accent. On the gable ends, log siding can replace whole logs for the same look, or you can use something entirely different.

RIGHT The potential for settling and insect damage, or the frequency with which you'll have to treat the exterior of your home will vary significantly from a desert region to an alpine one. Likewise, heavy snowfall or searing sun will dictate considerations in structure, orientation, and design.

• In the most efficient, compact floor plans, the rough plumbing shares a common wall whenever possible. Bathrooms are built back to back or stacked one on top of the other. Similar consideration is given to kitchen and laundry areas.

• Where do you live and how's the weather? There's no question that climate affects the spatial, structural, and functional requirements of a home. Wood needs to be protected from the weather, and snow loads are always a considera-

tion in affected climes. Likewise, moisture shouldn't be allowed to accumulate on top of log ends. Roof overhangs, covered decks and porches provide good protection from water falling from the sky, but don't overlook trouble spots from errant sprinklers.

• As in any home, the collective cost of windows, doors, and a myriad of other finish materials are the most dollar-consuming. Floors, fireplaces, wall partitions, cabinetry, appliances, and plumbing fixtures are only the beginning. Giant expanses of glass and odd-shaped windows are not only expensive but may dictate special structural considerations. A full masonry stone or rock fireplace can quickly add many thousands of dollars if you have to pay someone else to do it. All-wood floors will be more costly than wall-to-wall carpeting, and tile is pricier than vinyl flooring or Formica counters. Composition shingles will save dollars over cedar shakes. The danger of over-budgeting looms at every stage of construction, but it is at the finish stage where the money meter may dip perilously close to the red zone.

• If you're money-wise, you'll allow yourself plenty of time to shop around and compare various products. Consider costs, but don't overlook quality. You will want a product that can hold up under the rigors of your family's lifestyle. Ask yourself who will be installing what and for how much. If the answer to "who" is "you," then ask yourself what level of skill is required and if you are qualified. If you are not, then how long will it take to get qualified?

How Much Space Is Enough?

When we first open that door to our home vision and let our hopes, wants, and needs start spilling out onto paper, we begin to grapple with the concept of living space. We actually confront ourselves head-on as we identify those lifestyle choices that are most important to us. When we funnel our personal notions of small into a house plan, we chip away at the typical American standard for success. Real triumph lies in wanting less, consum-

ing less, and minimizing our debt load.

From the beginning it is best to examine all the motives behind your building plan. Does the possibility of resale creep into the design process and obligate you to add square footage or other amenities that you deem important to someone you've never met? How much have you paid for your land? Is costly property dictating that you overbuild to protect your investment? These concerns are not invalid, but be careful not to let them undermine your best efforts. For the same reason, you should take time to study any rules governing the ground you purchase. For instance, it is not uncommon for the powers that be in a subdivision to set minimum square footages for new homes.

How much space then do you need—or more appropriately, how much don't you need? As a family or individual, this is a good time to get out a pad and pencil and start a list. Put it all down, then stir it around. Distinguish between the "must haves," the "really wants," and the "would be nices," then stick your list in the freezer for a week or a month while you snoop around the neighborhood talking to friends, home-builder acquaintances, and all the helpful strangers you're sure to meet along the way.

• How will you use your home? Will this be your primary residence, a vacation retreat, guest house, or something else? Today, most log homes are built by people who plan on living there full-time for a long time. If that sounds like you, then the more time spent at the drawing board, the better.

• When you plan common living areas, an open design where rooms overlap can make individual spaces seem

BELOW As a building material, logs don't fit into molds that are tidy and predictable. Apart from the potential for shrinkage and settling, a builder has to have a steady hand when scribing drywall to logs. In this case, a length of rope provides good-looking cover where it may be needed most.

ABOVE This remodeled
mountain cabin epitomizes
great-room living in a small
space. While the house
includes a sunroom addition
and a tiny spare room in back,
owner Jane Whitson can close
those doors in the dead of
winter and be content in this
open and easy-to-heat space.

larger. This is the philosophy behind the
great-room approach, and many small
homes will feel suspiciously roomy when
you keep interior walls to a minimum. If
you do break up your living spaces, full
log walls will cost more and consume more
space than framed partitions.

• How large is your current family?
Will you be having more children or losing some to college or marriage? Will
elderly parents ever need to be cared for
in your home? If practical, plan to add on
later when time and money become available. Include drawings of the addition

with your current building plan so you
don't put a counter or plumbing wall
where you'll ultimately want an entryway.
Some families will construct a small log
building for practice, then live in it during the construction of their main home.
Down the road that first structure can be
converted to space for a shop, office, storage, guests, or . . .

• Will any member of your household be working out of your home? If so,
how big or quiet does their office need to
be? Consider all your nooks and crannies.
Can you squeeze space out of your living

room or master bedroom? How about a spacious walk-in closet? Will a loft, extra-wide landing, or corridor fill the bill?

• Having plenty of bathrooms and powder rooms is the luxurious norm in today's standard home, but are they always necessary? What is the personal cost of sharing the master bath with other members of your family or even your guests? Most small homes will not have extra rooms that serve the same function. The family room is the living room. The children's bedroom is the playroom. The breakfast nook is the dining room.

• I would venture that creating adequate storage space in any modest home is a challenge. We tend to collect and keep things we don't need and rarely use. To have extra room in a closet or kitchen cupboard is a noble goal, but too little storage space is distressing. Make the most of what you have by working on your organization skills. Consider making extra room in free-standing pieces of furniture, such as armoires or benches with under-seat compartments. Brainstorm at boat and RV shows, where maximizing usable space is a science; but if you find that you still can't handle the overflow, have a yard sale!

When you've finally identified your living spaces and roughed them together on paper, you'll need to pick up a ruler and draw your plan to scale. Stick to your upper limit for square footage by drawing your perimeter walls first, then sizing your rooms to fit inside. Identify each appliance, along with tubs, toilets, major pieces of furniture, electrical outlets, and switches. Keep in mind how large your logs will be so you don't make the mistake of calculating living space that will, in reality, be encroached upon by the walls. A few inches might not seem like much, but over the space of a whole house, inches turn quickly into feet. This goes double if your interior walls or partitions will be built with logs.

When you're sure you love your plan, show it off. Encourage critical review and constructive feedback. Perhaps you'll need to enlist the assistance of a professional to produce final working drawings. Chances are, you'll be required to get the whole works approved by an engineer.

Owner-builders are resourceful, persistent, and typically a little unconventional in their approach to building. When you operate under constraints of time, money, or experience, textbook precision may elude you. It is those very constraints, however, that can service individual desire and compel our greatest works.

BELOW As a Wyoming outfitter and guide, Jane Whitson lives year-round in this Buffalo Valley cabin built in the 1950s. With wood heat, propane appliances, and a gravity-feed water system, her sapling chinked-log hideaway is completely self-sufficient.

HANDS-ON HOUSES

There was a time when the average American family didn't have their own home unless they built it. I mean built it all, from the ground up. Okay, so way back in great-great-grandpa's day, dwellings weren't so complicated—they may not have had indoor plumbing, wiring, or central heat outside of the family hearth. Oh, the plain folk may have visited the blacksmith or local miller, but they didn't hire designers, contractors, subcontractors, and interior decorators. Most certainly, a bevy of grandpa's friends and neighbors pitched in to help. Of course, progress and technology have closed the doors and pulled the shades on great-great-granddad's world. It doesn't exist, and I'm not complaining. But with the comfort and convenience of progress and technology, families and individuals have become far more specialized and less self-reliant.

For the time-crunched masses who don't want or need to be hands-on homebuilders, then specialization and the services provided by experts are very good things. On the other hand, all this specialization promotes the assumption that you can't take on a task without formal training. That is, "if you're not a contractor, logsmith, plumber, or tile setter—don't try it."

You can live with that assumption if you want (in a rental home, perhaps), or you can turn the tables on that kind of thinking. More than training, you must have desire. So motivated, you can put technology and the modern world's extensive network of information to work for you. Use the experts and technicians for support. Hire them when you have to, but don't be afraid to march off the map into uncharted territory. Be wise, move cautiously, and expect to make a few mistakes along the way. Many jobs, like chinking, staining, flooring, or even roofing, are actually more tedious than they are high-tech, so make friends with patience and persistence. Other times, accessing the right tools or machinery will be the key to your success. Plan out each job ahead of time and think about the materials and equipment that you'll have to rent, borrow, or buy before you start.

All the homes in this chapter were built (or in one case, remodeled) with their own owners at the helm as designers and general contractors. Furthermore, each owner took on the additional work of different trades, sometimes with little or no previous experience. Like great-grandpa, these builders often called on knowing friends and willing family for advice or extra muscle. But more important, they all called on their own innate abilities to do, at least in part, what families have done before them for thousands of years.

Tom and Florence Blanchard
LOCATION: Bellevue, Idaho
SIZE: 2,000 sq. ft.
COST: $40,000 ($20/sq. ft.)
BUILDING TIME: 1977–1983
(and then some)
ADVICE: Don't bring out the beer
until the work is through!

In the 1960s and 1970s, traditional thinking and Mom's apple pie got put on a shelf while a generation of young people explored alternative value systems, life-styles, and house-building possibilities. Burdened by concerns for a troubled environment, and moved to action by the injustice of an unpopular war, millions of people embraced low-impact living, effectively launching a movement in this country that helped kindle new interest in log homes.

In the mid-seventies, Tom and Florence Blanchard, like so many of their peers, were self-described "back-to-the-landers." They were living in Mammoth

ABOVE New pine floors marked a move into the luxury zone for the Blanchards. Until 1990 they lived on plywood. Sometimes painted battleship gray and other times dark brown, that surface wasn't only ugly, it showed all the dirt. When new rough-cut pine boards arrived, Florence says it was like bringing home a Picasso. Sun-washed and textured, the golden wood with its circular saw marks was almost too precious to walk on.

Native, low-maintenance grasses surround the Blanchards' cordwood home, hiding a flood-conscious raised foundation.

Lakes, California, where it routinely snowed in mid-July. Wanting a garden but not willing to forego four seasons, they moved their family down in elevation to Bellevue, Idaho. It still snowed there, but summers were a little longer, and they could usually coax a tomato or two out of the garden.

They came to Bellevue with their children, the notion of building a mortgage-free home, and the *Mother Earth News*—a popular counterculture magazine for the self-reliant. When they first read about cordwood log homes, they were enamored. "What really happened," explains Tom, "is that we had always heated with wood. Winters in Mammoth Lakes were endless, and enormous stacks of dry logs by our fireplace meant warmth and security. We'd looked at those comforting log ends and thought, why not use them to build our walls."

They sent for the book mentioned in the article and made a list of the fifteen or so materials they would need, starting with mason's gloves and a kitchen knife

and wrapping up with log ends, sawdust, lime, and cement. In 1977 they purchased a three-acre site right on the Big Wood River, set up housekeeping in a trailer, and went to work. Making a point to use all indigenous materials, they bought local lodgepole pine. All their friends were invited over for a peeling party, then the wood was bucked, stacked, and left to dry for a year.

Wanting to know how much his log ends were going to shrink, Tom hauled samples to a grocery store in the nearby ski-resort town of Ketchum. He had them weighed on meat-market scales, then carted them back home for slow baking in his trailer oven. Once cooked, he measured and weighed them again, did some simple calculations, and *voila!*—science was served. (Well, sort of. Even today, calculating shrinkage is tricky business. The industry recognizes certain parameters, but climate, length of storage, and the wood itself makes precise estimates nearly impossible.)

The Blanchards drew up a 2,000-square-foot floor plan with more than half of the space allocated to one great big room. That, they say, is what happens when you design your home in a trailer—in the winter. Not ones to live "neat as a pin," they have filled the large space with more than twenty years worth of useful clutter. The rest of the house consists of three bedrooms, one family bath, and an enclosed, south-facing solar porch. To keep things rolling in the morning, sinks and medicine cabinets were installed in each bedroom.

Like so many do-it-yourself projects, building was a slow process for the Blanchards, and despite a short supply list, the required labor was even more intensive than they could have imagined. Still, cordwood construction is one of the easiest (if not tedious), least expensive, and most manageable approaches to alternative house building. You are basically working with firewood, so you don't need the kind of muscle or technology required to lay whole logs up on a wall. Each stick of wood is bedded in mortar, and some form of insulation is worked into the wall. In this cordwood house, posts and beams provide the skeletal framework. Shear is added with 4-by-4s braced diagonally against the posts and buried in the walls. Pearlite insulation was poured into air spaces in the middle. Despite their best attempts to avoid shrinkage, they had a little, and some of the logs wiggled away from the mortar. Tom has sealed many of the gaps with foam insulation, but when they get a good puff of wind, a little pearlite can still find its way into their food.

It was six years before the Blanchards sold their trailer and moved into their as-yet-unfinished home. In fact, that first summer they hadn't even gotten around to installing the doors. Then one night while camped out on the floor, they woke up to a dog fight in their living room. That got them moving on doors and windows, but some of the trim work and other details, like cabinet faces, may never be done.

"We've chosen a lifestyle with flexibility but not a lot of money," says Florence. And now that their children are grown, they have more freedom than ever. Gone are the goats, pigs, rabbits, and geese that they once raised for food. They still keep a garden and a few egg-laying hens, but they never did get around to replacing the family dog that died a couple of years back. With retirement and travel in mind, they will probably rent out their house in the near future, so they have installed a gas forced-air furnace. Before that, a woodstove provided all the heat they needed. Today's modern, super-insulated, double-walled this-and-that, says Tom, may be more efficient, but the temperature in this home has never fallen below 50 degrees Fahrenheit, even in the dead of winter. Besides that, these walls breathe, they transfer moisture, and, says Tom, "We like the way they look."

BELOW Tom's handmade front door opens to a cold entry that doubles as a mudroom and gear room. For the longest time, most of the walls in the house were white, but a trip to the colorful Southwest inspired a makeover with canary yellow paint and blue trim.

**Kent Eriksen and
Diane Mitsch Bush**
LOCATION: Steamboat Springs,
Colorado
SIZE: 1,700 sq. ft. plus 500 sq. ft.
of unfinished basement
COST: $94,000 ($55/sq. ft.)
BUILDING TIME: 1988–1991
ADVICE: Camp on your site,
experience it, and enjoy it
before you build.

BELOW Kent and Diane's home is built in the full-scribe Swedish tradition, where the bottom of one green log is carefully coped out to fit atop the next. As the wood dries, the logs shrink together to maintain a snug fit. To facilitate this process, logs are back-cut in "shrink-to-fit" corners. The decorative fascia was painted by a friend, and the design was applied with an imprinted European roller.

An owner-built home is a tangible extension of its makers. Both personal and revealing, it becomes a powerful affirmation of what matters. Kent Eriksen and Diane Mitsch Bush lead a lifestyle that balances creature comforts with a strong commitment to conservation and responsible living.

Kent and Diane have mostly lived in homes that were a little unconventional. Prior to this they were caretakers of an earth-berm home, and before that Kent actually lived in a homemade "tree house" tucked away in the aspen forest above Steamboat Springs. When they acquired their current fifteen-acre site, they weren't sure what they would build with. Then, while camping on the land and getting a feel for the sun and seasons, they learned of a partially built log shell that needed a

home. The former owner, knowing she was allergic to the natural oils occurring in pine, chose to build with aspen wood. When that didn't agree with her either, she was forced to abandon the project. Her hand-scribed log shell had sat in a lot for nearly a year when Kent found it, took home the dimensions, then stayed up all night redesigning the 27-by-27-foot box into a home.

The love of curves, a desire to squeeze in extra space under the eves, and the necessity of building a tall house inspired the home's extraordinary 35-foot-high, Hershey Kiss-shaped roof. On the darkest days of winter, the sun struggles to the top of the surrounding ridges, then barely scrapes along before dipping out of sight. Because the home utilizes passive solar heat and photovoltaics (utility-generated electricity is not available), being tall helps maximize the amount of sunlight reaching panels located near the peak of the roof. Winter also means serious snowfall, and it is not uncommon to get 380 inches annually. By raising the first floor above a daylight basement, Kent hoped to give the front door a head start in the race to stay above snow level.

Most of Kent's life has been spent building or working on bicycles. In the mid-seventies the challenge of riding down a mountain trail to work led Kent to experiment with fat tires on ten-speeds retrofitted with extra gears. What he was really doing was inventing the first mountain bike, and while there is still some debate as to who did what, Kent shares top honors in the Mountain Bike Hall of Fame. Bikes continued to direct the course of Kent's life, leading him to convert an old waste-burning sawmill "teepee" into the Sore Saddle Cyclery—Steamboat's old-

est bike shop. Since building and selling bikes for a living consumed his summers, house building took place in winter—a feat that made for high drama and still leaves Kent's friend and logsmith Thomas Wood shaking his head.

When Tom, Kent, and Diane brought the first load of logs to the site in November, it had snowed the night before. Not only was the road to their land steep and winding, but it stopped a quarter mile short of the building envelope. Diane says getting the logs to the site was an adventure, and the log skidder broke loose at the first serious curve. She's still not sure how they managed, but after the first load things seemed to go better. By December all the logs were up, a temporary coal-burning stove was cranking in the basement, and the building was sheathed in plastic so their work could continue.

As their own general contractors, Kent and Diane took the time to seek out good deals on house materials. Since most of their friends are in the building trade, they got "extras" off of job sites for nothing or next to it. All their doors and

ABOVE Most of the solar energy that heats this house streams in through the greenhouse. The small master bedroom is squeezed into the sunny third-floor dormer that Diane calls their "new improved tree house." They enjoy a tremendous view of the continental divide and a musical, predawn bird clock.

windows came from the salvage yard, and Kent dragged their curvy aspen banister out of the woods. "Custom" tiles in the guest bath are really just the basic stuff affixed with 75-cent decals. A brand new soapstone stove was a steal out of the classifieds. Kent installed it in a masonry enclosure that he built out of concrete block, chicken wire, and Ferro cement. The block work rooted in the basement acts as a heat sink, and the warm air that rises upstairs from either the stove or solar gain is recirculated to the basement via a metal chase running through the enclosure. They only need the stove in the coldest winter months, since their attached solarium soaks up more than enough heat.

Water is supplied to the home from a spring located 800 feet up the hill. A pipe buried in a hand-dug trench carries water to a 1,200-gallon holding tank. From there, gravity shoots the water to the house, so there is no need for pumps of any kind. Conservation-minded low-flow toilets and bath facilities are installed inside. Photovoltaic panels on the roof capture the sun's energy, then store it in a series of batteries. The house is wired with both AC and DC outlets. The computer and other large appliances operate off the AC current. Lights and smaller equipment run off DC, and there is a backup gas generator just in case. Kent and Diane have a propane-powered refrigerator, stove, and water heater. They also use a washing machine but line-dry their clothes summer and winter.

Kent and Diane's home works because they consciously choose to use less. They are rugged individuals who own cars but more often bike or ski the seven miles to work down 1,200 vertical feet of mountainside. The couple does not maintain their quarter-mile driveway in the winter, so they hand carry all their groceries in and haul their trash out through the snow. Both are highly committed to treading lightly on the earth, and they view their own home as a persuasive example of how it can be done without sacrificing real comfort.

LEFT Originally, the ceiling over the living area was open to the second story, but when Kent and Diane had trouble keeping heat in, they installed removable decking overhead during winter. In summer, they roll it back to create a cathedral-like place.

BELOW A hot bath is Kent's answer after a bike race or long backcountry ski. The tub, gifted by a friend, is perched on a cantilevered shelf that extends out from the back of the second floor. The overhang extends next door to the guest bedroom and is supported by a post on a screw jack that can be lowered as the building settles.

ABOVE Renee paid as she went, and by the time she was ready to landscape there was nothing left for pavers or nursery-bought plants. At first she tried a small patch of grass, but what the mice and rabbits didn't gobble up just withered away under scorching rays of the summer sun. After she tore it all out, it was the desert itself that gifted her a hardy garden and showed her the beauty and wisdom of transplanting and growing native flora.

Renee Farley
LOCATION: Palomino Valley, 25 miles north of Reno, Nevada
SIZE: 1,200 sq. ft., plus 340-sq.-ft. attached garage
COST: $100,000 ($76/sq. ft.)
BUILDING TIME: 1989–1991
ADVICE: There is truth to that old saying "It's not what you know but who." Oh, and don't forget to allow for settling.

One day in 1986 Renee Farley cut a picture of a log house out of a magazine and taped it to the fridge in her double-wide. For the next three years she fixed her sights on a new home far away from the congested shores of trailers and barking dogs. Finally, with her own plan and an iron will, she put her familiar life on hold for two years and took on a do-it-yourself project like no other.

At thirty-eight Renee was recently divorced, ambitious, and used to hard work. She was no stranger to the construction trade. Her own father had been a tile setter, her stepdad a contractor, and her ex-husband also an experienced builder. She herself had once made her living as a laborer, then gained more experience when she and her "ex" built stick-frame homes for both themselves and her parents. Log building would be something new, but that was exactly what Renee wanted—something new and "all me!"

Renee's parents allowed her to build on their 97-acre tract of solitude in Nevada's Palomino Valley. It is a place where sunlight and moonlight check the scurryings of diamond-studded snakes, twitching rodents, and chattering blue-winged birds. Beyond the desert mantle of juniper, Russian sage, and dry bones, a distant rise swallows up the nearest neighbor. When the light is just right, Renee can count seven waves of mountains rolling off the horizon. It is just the oasis that she had longed for.

After a lot of talk and careful research, Renee purchased a bare-bones log package from Alpine Log Homes in Victor, Montana, then hired her builder-friend Duane Steidley to work "with" her, not "for" her. She designed a house with 950 square feet of living space and an attached oversized garage. When there was more money and time, 250 square feet of that garage would be converted to a second bedroom and bathroom.

In January, with a fickle desert winter well under way, Renee broke ground. In the next several weeks she and Duane built the foundation from block to stem wall while holding down their full-time jobs. Renee says that with the ice and snow, her foundation seemed to take forever—making her infinitely happy that she had kept the design small. The logs arrived in May, along with a rented crane, a handful of eager friends, and baskets of home-packed victuals. Two long hard days later, Renee's pre-notched and numbered walls were set and spiked securely together.

Over the summer, building ceased while Renee worked on logistics and replenished her dwindling cash reserves. In those three months, sun and wind wicked more moisture out of the logs than she ever thought possible. Although the timbers had been harvested dead-standing, the arid desert climate and weight of the stacked logs caused her building to settle more than five inches! Renee had taken *none* of this into account, and she gasps out loud just thinking about the consequences had she installed doors and windows before the house had come down.

Working by Duane's side and with the occasional free help and advice of "expert" friends, Renee carried tools and wore the hats of a dozen different trades. Not only did she wield the logger's chain saw and the carpenter's hammer, but she stepped into the role of roofer, mason, electrician, plumber, and Sheetrocker. She

BELOW Dawn finds Renee and her dog up before the lizards and off into the hills. "The morning sun feels so good," she says, "sometimes it gives me goose bumps!" Each daily trek is actually a treasure hunt, and the booty she brings home all goes straight back into the landscaping around her home. Juniper root arbors like this one are Renee's homegrown solution for shade.

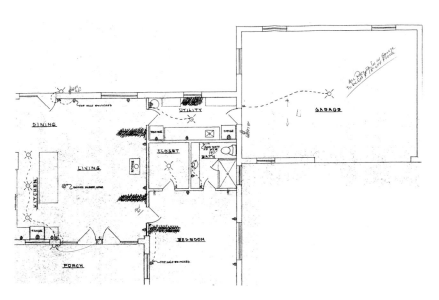

cut and set her own tile, laid down oak and flagstone floors, and learned to chink. Working into the night after her day job cleaning office buildings and from dawn to dusk on weekends, Renee poured all her energy, time, and money into her project. She attacked each new job with gusto but says, "It was reeeally hard work!" There were occasional setbacks too—like the morning she woke up to find her water line frozen solid. Even though she had buried her pipe to code, it hadn't been deep enough. She had to rent a backhoe to dig out all 1,200 feet of it. "That day I just cried and cried!" she says.

Other jobs, it seems, are never done. For more than seven years, Renee has kicked, carried, dragged, or rolled rocks, roots, skulls, and rusty desert artifacts out of the hills and into her yard. The paths around her home are pieced together with weather-beaten boards and stones, and all her shrubs and flowers are nurtured from hearty desert stock carefully hand-picked and transplanted. Renee's most distinctive works are the homespun juniper root arbors that she fashioned for shade. Her daughter calls them alien landings, but they are really fine examples of desert art and function blended carefully as one.

In retrospect, Renee believes it was more time-consuming to build with logs than with conventional lumber, but she adds,

ABOVE The "living" part of Renee's house is all concentrated in a great room under open-beam ceilings. Full log gables and the 40-foot purlins in the roof system added substantially to the price of her log package, but the house would not have felt the same without them. The house relies primarily on passive solar heat for warmth, and a bank of clerestory windows runs the entire length of the south side.

LEFT Outdoors is where Renee would rather be—hiking over the next ridge or collecting the first blooms of spring. Even before she undertook the building of her own log home, she would gather up the desert flora and bring it home to press and store. Those were the flowers she used between the glass of the kitchen cabinets.

LEFT Building a walk-in shower with glass blocks was easy but time consuming, says Renee. A half wall separates this master bathroom from the bedroom to preserve an open feeling in the rooms.

"It is so much more rewarding." Lulled into peaceful reflection by her protective logs and surrounded by the quiet calm of the desert, Renee feels content and safe from the crazy confusion of Reno's neon lights and over-amped tourists. The smell of a desert rain or the violent spectacle of lightning bolts dueling on the horizon tickle all her earthly senses. "Just maybe," says Renee, "I was born a hundred years too late," but to her, hard work and a blanket of solitude are easy companions.

ABOVE The "almost plain" architecture of the Macleans' home makes it feel more like an old homestead. Early on, they shrunk their L-shape floor plan to a rectangle when they learned how much labor was concentrated in the log corners. Fewer notches, less roof, and a smaller foundation all meant added savings.

Janis and Rod Maclean
LOCATION: Reedpoint, Montana
SIZE: 1,543 sq. ft. with sunroom
COST: $60,000 ($39/sq. ft.)
BUILDING TIME: August 1989–
October 1990 (plus years of
finish work)
ADVICE: If you want it
up yesterday—don't!

Janis Maclean may have been born and bred a city girl, but she spent her childhood riding roughshod with the pretend cowboys and Indians of her Wild West fantasies. She was a cowgirl at heart, and it was horse lore, *Bonanza* on TV, and tales of the legendary sharpshooter Annie Oakley that left indelible marks on her heart. Having grown up in Toronto, Canada, she never expected to live in her own log house in an American state whose entire population wasn't half that of her metropolitan hometown. Yet, having discovered Montana cow country with her husband Rod, there was never any question that they would build with logs. In a way, for Janis it was like coming full circle from fantasy to reality.

Both consider it a near miracle that they managed a home at all. In the beginning Janis was a waitress and pregnant with their second child. Rod was employed seasonally and their bank savings were meager at best. They did, however, have forty-seven acres of Montana countryside, a passionate desire to build a small manageable house, and enough gumption to put it all together. Janis says that Rod is a handy fellow, but he went strictly by the book, while, as a fine arts major, she was led by her keen sense of aesthetics. The result was a partnership where fact collided with fantasy often enough to keep them on track and conscious of their own limitations in the building process. They determined early on that they could dig the foundation but would get help with the log work and roof system. They produced the floor plans, acted as their own general contractors, and did the lion's share of the labor and finish work. Janis even handcrafted her own Molesworth-style log furnishings along with the rugs, deerskin lamp shades, and picture frames.

It wouldn't be fair to say that the Macleans' design wasn't partly defined by their budget, but for Janis, it was a much deeper respect for the place, its people, and its history that made building small so important. The people who first home-steaded nearby were ranchers, and so are their neighbors today. There is hardship and the money isn't always good, but they are rich in spirit. The land is more than their anchor, it's a part of them. Only now she says, there are developers promoting rural sprawl on every hill at every turn.

"We didn't want our house to be another pockmark that overshadowed its place. The land had to be the most important part of what we did here, and when people came to visit I wanted them to say 'Oh, what a beautiful *place*'—not 'Oh, what a beautiful *house*.'"

Respect mingled with an intruding sense of guilt kept Janis and Rod up at night thinking of ways to keep their home small without sacrificing the comforts of year-round living. They wanted the house to appear smaller on the outside than it actually was, and decided on a 26-by-36-foot, story-and-a-half rectangle with an

BELOW Janis fell in love with the look of Molesworth furniture, but when she saw the $60,000 price tag on a reupholstered set of the famous craftsman's work, she decided she would have to build her own. So she did—along with nearly all the rest of the log furniture, rag rugs, picture frames, and deerskin lamp shades in the house!

RIGHT Using log guru B. Allan Mackie's how-to books, Rod built the "Rockinghorse" bunkhouse with no previous experience in log-home construction. The walls were built with untreated telephone poles and hoisted into place with the help of Rod's small farm tractor. The door was salvaged from the original homestead on the property.

FAR RIGHT TOP Janis built the stone wall in the entryway, and the couple carved the home's birthday in the summer beam overhead. At ground level, the floors are laid atop a radiant-heat system fueled by a wood-burning furnace. With a price tag nearing that of a small car, the furnace was one of the most expensive items in the house. With plentiful free wood out back, the system will pay for itself over time.

FAR RIGHT BOTTOM Rod and Janis put a full bath on the main floor next to the guest bedroom that will one day be their own when stairs become a nuisance. In keeping with the economy of small design, this bathroom sits directly below the second-floor family bath. This design consideration, along with the placement of the stairs, strongly influenced the layout of the rest of the house.

oversized front porch. However, if visitors were fooled by the outside appearance, then the inside should be surprisingly spacious. The living, kitchen, and dining rooms were loosely defined into one great room. Every square inch of floor and wall space was precious. The owners had a radiant-heat floor installed not only for comfort and efficiency but because that would eliminate the need for floor vents, baseboard heaters, or ductwork. Windows were few, relatively small, and carefully placed so that the family's few sentimental pieces would not feel cramped inside.

Rod had every intention of laboring alongside their logsmith, Jeff Pederson, during what he deemed "the fun part of the project!" In the past few years Rod had gotten out all of his log-building books and had constructed his own one-room, round-log bunkhouse and a hewn piece-en-piece workshop. Jeff tested their working relationship by briefly apprenticing Rod on another home project he was completing. Success! Rod polished up his technique, and the wages he would have earned were deducted from Jeff's bill to them.

In late August of 1989, Jeff and his wife Eileen came to live in the Macleans' sparse bunkhouse. They would rough it there for the two months it took to notch and stack the log walls. Likewise, Janis, Rod, and their toddler son, Tyler, lived on-site in a shabby but affordable twenty-year-old double-wide.

Janis laughs when she thinks back to life in that mouse-infested tin box. Her second son, Lawson, was born that winter—nine months before the family would move into their new home. She recalls, "If the wind blew, you could see

waves in the toilet! When it got cold, blankets hung to insulate the windows would freeze right to the glass, and we'd have to bundle up the boys in parkas just to feed them breakfast."

Rod used his tractor to excavate the foundation, while Janis kept the job site as clean as Jeff had ever seen. Later on, and getting more pregnant by the day, she would work from scaffolding to clean, bleach, and stain all the logs before the chinking crew arrived. Rod did the finish work on the roof and nailed on all the shakes.

With the log shell under roof, the work had only just begun. Baby Lawson arrived in January, leaving Janis with two

small boys to cater to while she and Rod caulked, stained, painted, sanded floors, and hand-adzed all the trim boards. Janis also single-handedly picked and hauled tons of rocks out of the creek and field—enough to fill all their masonry needs. The Macleans hired masons to design their firebox and build the rock chimney outside, but Janis did all the rock work at the base of the foundation and on the fireplace inside.

By October of 1990, although the kitchen wasn't finished, they moved in. Over the course of the next few years, they finished the interior, landscaped their little clearing, and built a tiny sunroom off their dining area. Rod planted a garden large enough to keep their family and the deer in vegetables. He says, "We can't keep the deer out, so we feed them in the summer, then eat them in the winter!" Janis says she used to be a vegetarian, but now she's just part of a natural cycle. She and Rod have tremendous respect for the abundant wildlife, and they don't waste much of anything. Even the hides are used by Janis for her handmade deerskin lamp shades.

Now Janis can barely describe how proud she is of their home. When a forest fire threatened to take it all last summer, Janis wondered if they could do it again. Her answer: "Of course. How could we ever settle for anything less?"

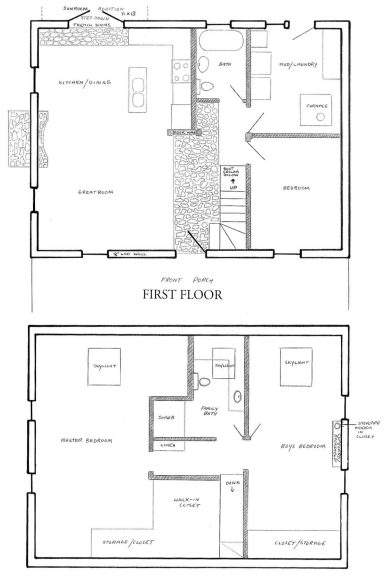

FIRST FLOOR

SECOND FLOOR

ABOVE The walls stop at a height of just ten feet. Only one and a half courses of logwork carry through to the second floor. Where the logs stop, the sloping roof begins, in essence making the upstairs one big attic. To change the pace of things, the Macleans used Sheetrock to set off the timber-frame construction of the roof and make the rooms seem brighter and bigger. There is no heat upstairs, so south-facing skylights let in light and warmth. A rope ladder dangles from a makeshift "tree house" secured in the timbers above the boys' bedroom.

Bill and Nondi Phelps
LOCATION: Bitterroot Valley,
Montana
SIZE: 1,700 sq. ft.
COST: $65/sq. ft.
BUILDING TIME: 1989, six months
ADVICE: Design to fit your site, and
don't overlook outdoor living areas.

BELOW The Montana sun shines until 10:30 P.M. most summer nights. When Bill and Nondi aren't working, they spend nearly every daylight hour outdoors. With twenty acres and eight horses there is plenty to do. "Basically, we just fence the animals out of the yard, then live in it," laughs Bill.

Back in the early eighties, Bill Phelps sold chunks of Colorado countryside—land best viewed from a rocking chair on a log-house porch. So inspired, he took on a log-home dealership, selling property along with a cabin to put on it. He went to work for a machine-milled log-home company, then eventually gave up real estate to sell kit homes full time. He worked with Rocky Mountain Log Homes for

nearly nine years and helped them set up a sister company to market handcrafted homes. In 1989 Bill and his family built their own manufactured log house from a package purchased from Bill's employer. As a company salesman, he got a special rate on a complete kit that included house logs, timbered floor joists, ridge beams, rafters, windows, and doors. The Phelpses' design is a modified version of a standard floor plan provided by the log producer. Most companies have cataloged their most popular plans and can easily customize them for little or no extra money.

Back in 1989, the Phelpses' 1,700-square-foot-house package would have retailed for around $32,000. Today, Bill estimates the same package would cost nearly twice that amount. Most owner-builders find they save money by purchasing a less-complete kit, then searching out their own deals on items like doors and windows. But as a company man, Bill was already saving money, and he would use

ABOVE When you buy a machine-milled log home, you'll find countless wall styles and log profiles to choose from. These walls are chinkless Swedish cope with saddle-notched corners. The horizontal interfaces of the logs are triple sealed, with plywood splines and foam gaskets. The corners are filled with more foam, then caulked.

ABOVE When the handcrafted guest-house arrived pond-side in 1994, a second septic permit was out of the question due to high groundwater. Necessity led the Phelpses to install an electric toilet that dehydrates and burns waste at the push of a button. They have only to empty the ashes.

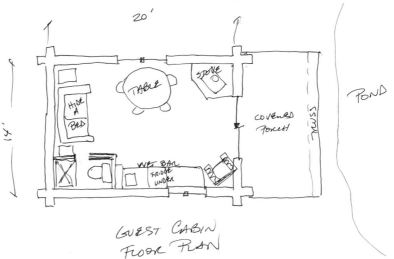

GUEST CABIN
FLOOR PLAN

The one-room guest cabin is only 440 square feet, so everything is scaled way down. Narrow shelves scribed into the logs display the dinner dishes, and the tiny copper sink is good for washing a plate or two at a time.

his home as a model for regional sales.

For Bill and his wife Nondi, siting the house was every bit as important as the floor plan. They spend all their decent-weather days outdoors, and they didn't want to fry in the afternoons on west-facing decks. They also used the orientation of the sun and house to control snow loads in winter. "This place," says Bill, "was not designed so much to be lived in as it was to be lived around." Basically, they just cook and sleep inside, unless it's barbecue season. Then they just sleep inside—sometimes.

In season, the decks out back ease into a shady place laced with birdsong and the delights of summer. Water diverted from an irrigation ditch on the property courses through one pond, then under a willow-draped bridge into another. Water toys, floats, and fishing poles are never far from hand. A comfortable mishmash of old stumps and benches curl around a fire ring that overlooks the water. At sunset, Burl the bullfrog sits near the bank and pines for his gal, while eleven-pound trout spin circles across their dinner table. It all feels suspiciously like summer camp!

The water table is so high on the property that Nondi says she just sticks things in the ground and they grow. By the same token, the floodplain laps at their doorstep. Building smart, they raised the home several feet above grade. Earth excavated from their ponds was used to build up the yard around the foundation.

In the early days, milled-home production was assured, while a craftsman-built cabin could take a long time. To some extent this is still true today, but there are a lot more handcrafters out there, including Pioneer Log Homes, the sister company Bill helped found. In 1991, Bill began to market these new hand-peeled and notched homes with gusto. For three years running, he outsold all his peers. In reward, the company gifted him a one-room guest cottage. It was planted pond-side in 1994, and Bill poked around for eight months on the finish work.

Today he works for Custom Log Homes, another handcrafter in the Bitterroot Valley. He can tell you nearly anything you want to know about the different building methods. There are advantages to both, but, all things being equal, it is easier to construct a milled home, since precision-cut joinery fits together smoothly and many of the building components are interchangeable. This method is more forgiving and less labor intensive. Milled homes are also less expensive, but Bill says the pricing gap between the two seems to be narrowing nowadays—particularly for large fancy homes with complicated roof systems. He warns that a manufactured home requires solid log-building know-how. As for handcrafted log homes, the truth is Bill has picked up his ball and moved into that camp, lured, he says, by the wood itself, handworked, textured, and natural.

LEFT Bear, the dog, poses in front of this little guest house stove resurrected from an ancient cabin in the historic mining town of Virginia City. Montanans first discovered gold in that town, but today's treasure hunters have other things in mind. The slate for the hearth also came from there and is framed by wood found drifting in the river.

Al and Anne Posnack
LOCATION: Central New Hampshire
SIZE: 600 sq. ft.
COST: $10,000 ($16/sq. ft.)
BUILDING TIME: 1982–1986
ADVICE: Expand your planning
horizon. Consider your wants
and needs in several years and
build to accommodate them as time,
money, or necessity dictates.

"For Sale." It was just a little sign tacked up on a tree in the woods above the lake, but it would mark one of those experiences in life that you don't plan until you get there. The sign had caught Al Posnack's eye at a time when things were getting cramped on the twenty-four-foot sailboat where he spent the weekends with his new wife, Anne, and their three children from mixed marriages. Never mind that there wasn't money in the budget. He would show the land to Anne while wooing her over with wine and a gourmet, home-packed picnic lunch. Well, it worked, he chuckled, despite the fact that his dessert (leftover chocolate mousse) turned out to be cold congealed gravy.

The family bought the land and considered building a tent platform or maybe a small framed bunkhouse with an out-

RIGHT The Posnacks had visited a lot of homes to collect ideas. They borrowed favorite features, such as these built-in bunk beds tucked up against the kitchen wall. With a family of five and plenty of friends, they wanted as much sleeping space as possible. Now as many as ten people can overnight comfortably in their 600-square-foot cabin.

door privy. There was no grand plan, no thoughts of running water or electricity. Then they discovered that outhouses were prohibited on the property. Since an expensive septic system and a tent platform seemed silly, they started investigating small home ideas. That's when Al and Anne discovered logs and decided to combine a log cabin with a small post-and-beam addition. They would do 90 percent of the work themselves, and Anne jokes that for the next four years, Al headed into the bathroom every morn-ing with a different book in his hand.

After a year and a half of planning, they ordered a log-home package—not a kit, emphasizes Al. Though their green logs were sawn on three sides, they came in random 12-to-16-foot lengths. The pieces were not precut or numbered. The truck arrived with the logs, dumped them in a pile, and took off.

Anne had no building experience while Al had made some country furniture and a couple of birdhouses. "Early on," says Al, "I was discouraged by our

ABOVE Set on concrete piers, the Posnack's "Mouse House" is nestled into a natural clearing in their woods.

pace. We could only work on weekends, and it seemed to be going so slowly." The solution, he says, was actually simple. "If something took too long, we decided that our time estimate had been off—not the 'doing' part. And if we just reminded ourselves that we were building because we enjoyed the process as much as we would enjoy the product, then we didn't feel as rushed." Al adds that "after a long week at the office, it was such good therapy to beat the brains out of a bunch of ten-inch spikes."

When tools kept getting lost on the wooded lot, they spray painted them fluorescent red. A 2-by-4 with a spike protruding from one end became a handy lever to help wedge the butt of one log up tightly against the side of another. Everybody had a different suggestion on the best sealant to use between the logs, and after weeding through half a dozen expert opinions, they decided on two layers of sticky-backed foam stripping. By the end of the first year the log walls were up, the roof on, and a few windows installed. Anne had survived the blow from a hammer dropped directly onto her head from two stories up, but nearly as impressive, she could now expertly wield that tool along with all the others in her box!

By the end of summer number two, the cedar-shaked, post-and-beam addition was in place, along with the wiring and plumbing. Al explains that the cabin is basically a three-season retreat, but the plumbing is designed so that all the pipes flow downhill to a central point. The whole system can be drained by turning a couple of valves. If they do want to make a winter foray, they can heat up the cabin in a matter of hours, turn on the water, then later, re-drain their pipes and walk

LEFT Al says plenty of their friends came by to help, but two of the hardest workers were pushing eighty. Both are gone now, but when the family recalls those days, Al remembers "Harry Parker, always perched on top of the wall despite a steady diet of whatever he kept in that paper bag, and Hy Bergstein, with his blacksmith's hands, boundless energy, and a steady stream of how-to advice." In the end, all their friends signed a board that hung on a tree at the site. That wonderful memento now hangs just right of the window in the living room.

safely away without a lot of fanfare.

During the third and fourth years, built-ins, finished floors, trim work, and furniture were readied. Then they stopped working. There was no discussion, no dancing on the tables, and no railing on the loft. The cabin was unceremoniously transformed from weekend project to vacation getaway. For the next ten years, bare bulbs hung from the ceiling and hammers stayed in the toolbox. They didn't pick them up again until they heard we were coming.

If they had it all to do over again (and they would, says Al) they would have included a deck and screened porch. A few simple layout changes early on would have made it easy. Not so now. Also, he advises, the closer you live to your project, the better. A two-hour commute, with all the unpacking, settling up, and repacking took a big bite out of their short weekends. Is it finished? Al says no, and maybe it never will be—but having evolved from a tent platform, their plumbed and wired getaway is absolute nirvana.

Near the end of the project a friend asked the family how they knew they could do it. After a lot of thought Al determined, "we just never stopped to ask."

ABOVE None of the recycled windows in the Posnack cabin are alike. Worked in as building progressed, mismatched windows, painted doors, and other special touches give this cabin its cheery personality.

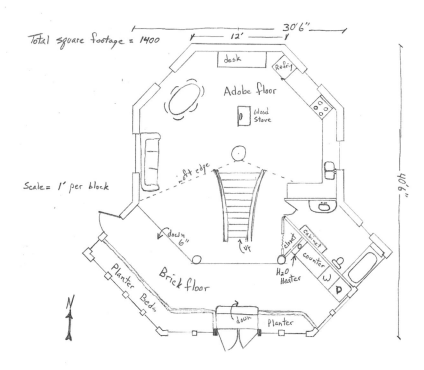

Total square footage = 1400

30'6"

12'

desk

Refrig

Adobe floor

Wood Stove

Scale = 1' per block

loft edge

down 6"

up

closet

cabinet

counter

H₂O Heater

W D

Brick floor

Planter Beds

down

Planter

N

9'04"

Tony Prendergast and Sally Kane
LOCATION: Crestone, Colorado
SIZE: 1,400 sq. ft.
COST: $25,000 ($18/sq. ft.)
BUILDING TIME: 1990–1994
ADVICE: Look for land without
the constraints of building codes,
and rely on local ingenuity.

Local ingenuity. It should come naturally, and yet, Tony Prendergast believes the wisdom of building with local materials and skills has largely been lost to contemporary homebuilders. This is partly because people have more money and depend less on shared energy and resources. But more significantly, he says, traditional building concepts have largely been zoned and coded out. In most communities, someone else will try to tell you what you need and how to build it. If you can free yourself from controlling bank loans, architects, and building codes, then Tony believes you can shape a home that reflects the way you live rather than constructing a home that, in fact, shapes you.

When Tony and his wife, Sally Kane, started out, they had less than $100 saved between them and no possibility of borrowing money for house construction. Their solution: patience, hard work, and local ingenuity. They would design a passive solar house—something two could build using native materials. Logs were cheap and available since Tony could shag what he needed down from the hills behind their property. The wood, properly harvested, is eminently renewable and nontoxic. You don't need fancy machinery, and while some skill is required, the concept is neither tricky nor complicated. And, explains Tony, wood performs so beautifully, staying warm in winter and cool in summer. A log house will outlast a frame house and is more resistant to fire. Well built, a home could conceivably stand for hundreds of years.

Though Tony primarily teaches wilderness survival and exploration courses through Outward Bound, he first tasted of log building shortly after moving to the remote mountain community of

LEFT Tony and Sally have a dramatic high-desert lot plunked down between weather-gripped mountains and a calming expanse of western plain. The hills beyond their property yielded tall, straight, dead-standing trees that Tony snatched from the bottom of steep ravines or floated across lakes and beaver ponds. All told, he has $1,000 in their logs, counting firewood permits, work gloves, truck gas, and breakfast at the diner for any friend willing to help.

BELOW Handcrafted ladderlike stairs are defined by stringers of curving logs. There are no railings here or elsewhere. The children, having navigated precarious heights since toddlerhood, are nimble as mountain goats. The great room floor is built from lightweight adobe called "scoria." Paw prints frozen in time retell the story of an unplanned but spirited cat-and-dog chase over the freshly poured surface.

ABOVE Upstairs, partitions
stop far short of the ceiling,
permitting heat and light to
circulate freely while dividing
the living space into two
sections: the loosely defined
master bedroom pictured here
and a room for the children
next door. Colorful fabric in
the doorway affords some
privacy for sleeping, but
around the corner, a book-
lined balcony opens to the
living area below.

RIGHT Log vigas supporting
the roof radiate from a central
post like spokes in a wheel.

Crestone, Colorado. Having been asked
to build a 400-square-foot, scribed-log,
Navajo-style "hogan," he and a friend
went to work using an article out of *Fine
Homebuilding* as their guide. It was that
building experience that led Tony to design a similar structure for his family. Not
only is the eight-sided design extremely
stable, but it's a geometry that works well
with logs. Shorter lengths are required in
each section, so the logs are lighter and
easier for a husband-wife team to wrangle
up skids and onto the walls.

Tony did invest in a winch for his
truck and used it to log and haul his trees
to the site. Later, as multiple courses
reached skyward, the winch was put to

work dragging logs from the pile and up
onto walls approaching sixteen feet in
height. He rented a backhoe to help hoist
the twenty-two-foot center pole into place.
Then he again used his winch and old
climbing ropes to set sixteen log vigas ra-
diating out from the top of the post like
spokes in a wheel to form the structural
supports of the roof.

The house is built to be as energy
efficient as Tony and Sally knew how.
While most people tend to insulate their
homes from earth below, this couple chose
to lay their adobe floors directly on the
sandy ground, then isolate that chunk of
ground from the earth outside their walls.
They hand-dug a perimeter trench twelve

inches wide and four feet beneath grade—safely below the frost line. In that trench, concrete weight-bearing columns were poured on footers at each of the eight corners. In between the columns, standard forms were built and filled with pumicecrete, a highly insulative mixture of lightweight lava rock and Portland cement. Log walls were erected on top of the columns and pumicecrete walls, but the adobe floors were laid directly on the dry sandy soil. As a result of the perimeter foundation wall, the earth under the house and, thus, the temperature inside never drop below fifty degrees Fahrenheit, even though Crestone goes on record many winter days with the coldest temperatures in the country.

Through four years of intermittently building and working for wages, Tony, Sally, and their two children lived in phase one of construction—a 200-square-foot log cabin intended as a shop. They had no plumbing or hot water and cooked on a small gas-burning stove. The kids slept under the raised bed. Though that small space was trying, the couple was not deterred from designing an open floor plan to maintain family togetherness and create a welcome gathering spot for friends. Though fairly remote, guests seem drawn to this warm casual home, and stories and ideas flow from the myriad of visitors who come and go.

This family has never wanted a house that looked like it was dropped from a Chicago suburb, and they have worked hard to integrate their home and their lives into their landscape. People like to say they are environmentalists, says Tony, but when you don't participate in your environment, you don't know how to love it nor how deep that love can go.

At an elevation of 8,400 feet, the high-desert ecosystem is more fragile than it looks. Once disturbed, the sandy soil is reluctant to bear new fruit. Tony and Sally have spent years building up the soil around their home to grow a garden and coax along native grasses and young trees. They hunt meat for their table, keep goats, chickens, and turkeys in the yard, and brew their own beer. There has been sacrifice through the years, but, says Tony, lessons learned about living simply day by day have brought their family especially close. They feel grounded here and believe they have a quality of life that is both rich and fulfilling.

ABOVE One of the best things about designing your own home is the freedom to borrow and create without constraint. Though we were influenced by early Forest Service architecture, we weren't bound by any particular criteria. Combining nostalgia with other whimsical elements admired from a house in our first book, *American Log Homes,* we added a certain storybook character befitting our site. A detached garage was eventually built on the foundation in the foreground.

Art and Cindy Thiede
LOCATION: Ketchum, Idaho
SIZE: 1,800 sq. ft.
COST: $108,000 ($60/sq. ft.)
BUILDING TIME: 1986
ADVICE: Safety first!

Log home fever was something Art caught back in 1979. He had come off a Lincoln Log high as a kid, and it was the doing part that left him searching for log dogs, drawknives, and chain saws. His enthusiasm was contagious, and we found ourselves caught up in an exciting time of architectural reinvention. Art went to log-building school in British Columbia, then returned home to re-create a landmark cabin for the Lake Tahoe Historical Society. With one project down, he was hot to do another, and it wasn't long before we were settled in Idaho's Wood River

Valley, with a chunk of ground, house plans, a brand-new chain saw, and a hefty bank loan.

"We were out there," says Art, "and when that logging truck dumped its first load, I was still trying to calculate the interest on our loan." Even though Art had built once before, this would be our first project from drawing board to doorbell. In the beginning, there were lots of what-if questions, and we hadn't even gotten out of the starting gate when Art spied his brand-new chain saw totally demolished under the first load of logs. "I knew

then," says Art, "that this was going to be a long strange trip, indeed."

After constructing the foundation, the task was to get poles and highlines up over the building to help maneuver logs onto the walls. Art selected a pair of 45-foot logs from the deck and attached a 15-foot cross tie near the top of each one. A friend with a crane set them into 5-foot holes at either end of the foundation. What happened next was one of the scariest things Art has ever done in construction. He had to rig a cable through the snatch block on top, but his longest

BELOW A partially enclosed wood-burning stove separates the living spaces in this open floor plan. The stove includes a handy self-cleaning flue. A cable, attached via a pulley block in the chimney cap, runs down the inside of the flue to a stainless-steel wire brush. When you crank the handle above the stove, the brush moves up and down, scraping away creosote buildup inside.

BELOW Logwork that supports the second-story floor figures prominently into the visual impact of this home's interiors. In the kitchen, a work island and breakfast bar ground a structural post.

ladder was still five feet too short. He recalls, "I had to leave the ladder and shinny the rest of the way up the pole. From there I belly-crawled to the end of the cross tie. The post swayed with every move, and it was forty dizzy feet down to the ground!" Getting back to earth was even trickier. He quickly began to appreciate why so many pioneer cabins were only one story high, and as soon as the house was finished, Art vowed to get a crane.

Art and I are hooked on nostalgia, so any house we design will reflect some distant bit of history. This home was partly influenced by the look of early Forest Ser-

vice and National Park Service architecture. During the Great Depression in the 1930s, the government created the Works Progress Administration to employ tens of thousands of out-of-work Americans in programs that built much of our country's infrastructure. Bridges, roads, airstrips, and public places were produced by the thousands, including some of the most-visited log lodges, cabins, and lookout towers on our public lands. Buildings were often finished in green and dark brown, and those familiar colors link this post-and-beam design to some of its more recent forebears.

LEFT A deck and a sunroom extend the living space for all seasons.

Many of the early Forest Service buildings also had similarly steep-pitched roofs. Such a feature would accommodate heavy snow loads better in areas where winter visitors were more likely to have wings or four legs than a shovel. A steeper pitch transfers snow loads more readily to the walls and lessens the strain on the roof structure. The improved ability to shed snow and water also prolongs the life of shakes or shingles.

We finished our first house in less than a year, but before we ever moved in, a young family fell in love with the place and offered to buy it for a price that covered wages and erased our debt. *What?!*

We had put so much of ourselves into this home that I couldn't believe we would consider selling before we'd even carted our first load of groceries across the threshold. Art felt differently. It was the process itself that gratified him. Hanging off the end of a wobbly cross tie forty feet above the ground was an exhilarating challenge! Unlocking the secrets of logs along with his own innate ability to build and create was more than he could stand. He was ready to build again but not for somebody else. He would retain the brushes and the paint, and conjure up another design to feed what had become an insatiable urge—and we did.

ABOVE We built our house on-site with wood purchased from a local logger. Using a portable band-saw mill, Art shaped everything from the wall logs and corner posts to the mantel over the fireplace. "I felt like a diamond cutter hunched over my wheel. These gnarly old logs were my stones, and I got to turn them into gems," says Art. On the walls, a gray weathering stain makes for virtually maintenance-free exteriors.

Art and Cindy Thiede
Thiede Homestead
LOCATION: Wood River Valley, Idaho
SIZE: 3,000 sq. ft.
COST: $75/sq. ft
BUILDING TIME: 1992–1993
ADVICE: If fantasy is part of your reality, then dream and build away.

Stirred by the grit of families that tilled rural America, and saddened by the gradual passing of the small family-owned farm, Art and I have worked a bit of homestead history into our current house and barn. Traditional farmhouse architecture, the simple genius of the water-pumping windmill, and the nostalgic lean of ancient weather-beaten barns are remembered in our small collection of new log buildings and old farmyard junk.

Our home is patterned after a traditional building style called the "tri-gabled ell." Thousands just like it were built in small towns and farm-belt communities between the late 1800s and mid-1930s.

Of course, most were stick built, so we tried something new. Instead of round brown logs, our farmhouse begged a clean look with trim corners. Our budget suggested that we build as efficiently and economically as possible. The perfect solution was to saw the logs flat on two sides, then butt them into posts at the corners instead of hewing out intricate notches. This form of construction is actually called *piece-en-piece* and was introduced by the French Canadians when America was still in the cradle.

Since this approach is less labor intensive than notched-log building, it went up faster. There were no interlocking corners to dictate log coursing, so entire wall sections could be built at once rather than having to build around the perimeter, one course at a time. We also got by with fewer lineal feet of wood because we didn't need to project the log ends beyond the corners. Finally, since the coursing of logs ascends in a level plane, we didn't have to deal with half courses and unequal wall-plate elevations.

BELOW Attention to detail and little extras add to the farmhouse character. Sage green kitchen cabinets are faced with common beaded board, then painted and rubbed for a been-used look. Overhead, honey-colored beams contrast with whitewashed logs. Beadboard wainscoting skirts the bottom of all the interior walls, and we've incorporated painted baseboard trim and crown molding throughout.

TOP RIGHT The second-story floor consists of wood decking laid over exposed timbers. Since you can't hide plumbing in this kind of floor, we built a raised platform for our vintage cast-iron tub.

FACING PAGE An exposed southwest-facing patio can be too blazing hot to enjoy in summer. Ours was—so we enclosed it with lattice supported on a framework of post and beams. A thick wall of fast-growing chokecherry bushes planted around the perimeter provides extra shade and protection from the wind.

LOWER RIGHT A Rumsford fireplace in the living room is framed by a new built-to-look-old surround and mantel. Art fashioned it from wood milled on his band saw, then applied several coats of paint and an antique crackle finish. Brick is used around the fireplace inside, while outside, the full-masonry chimney is faced with cultured stone—a sculpted, lightweight concrete product that is less labor intensive to install and nearly indistinguishable from the real thing.

To accommodate some very tall second-hand windows and give our traditional floor plan a more open feel, we created ten-and-a-half-foot ceilings, then whitewashed our interior walls. The logs were stacked with wide irregular spaces in-between, and because we left them round on top and bottom, we have wavy chink lines reminiscent of those found in traditional hewn-log construction.

In designing our home we weren't necessarily trying to be authentic, but we did want to invite the memory of another place or time. We coupled the traditional lines of the house with things like shutters, a cupola, window boxes, and a mom-and-pop front porch. Then adding a little

BELOW A friend's century-old, two-story log dairy barn with a braced rafter roof inspired Art to build something like it on our property. He found construction details in a university publication, then built the trusses on the ground before lifting them into place. In our cupola, the very bell that once summoned local children to class over a hundred years ago is still at work.

Victorian flair, we splurged on high-grade "fish scale" shingles for the roof and gable ends.

Typically, an old house wouldn't have an attached garage, so Art didn't want one. But the fact is we live in snow country, and I still get to cart around the kids and groceries. Art finally agreed but tried to play the addition down by adding extra windows to make it look more like a wing of the house. He custom-built two handsome sets of garage doors and designed them to swing out instead of up. To automate them, he simply modified

standard automatic garage-door hardware. They work just fine, and if you don't count Art's labor, they were far less expensive than installing overhead doors with the beefy old-time look we were striving for. The drawback is that after a snowstorm nobody goes anywhere until we clear a path behind our doors. A snow-melt system in the driveway would be one sure fix, but for now, an alarm clock and John Deere work just fine.

Whenever Art and I head out on the back roads and blue highways of America, we get sentimental over the lonely clumps

of paint-peeled houses and swaybacked barns that still hold court in great big dusty fields. Those old barns and occasional windmills, some still squawking in the breeze, trigger a mixture of emotions that are oddly comforting.

Our windmill is a relic from the late 1800s. Some mills are still in use today, but rural electrification rendered most obsolete, except as targets for bored farm boys and their trusty .22s. Our mill had been worked over when we found it, and Art completed the restoration by building the tower on which it stands. It isn't set up to pump water since we couldn't afford a second well, but with the addition of a sucker rod and a hole, it surely could.

The inclusion of a full basement increased our square footage by a third. Although basements are a cost-effective way to make space, this home could be built without one. Since Art and I both have offices here, the extra room has been useful, but we guarantee that when you add space, you'll fill it up with stuff you can live without.

When we look at our creation, we don't just see a house; we see a homestead. As owner-builders, we have something here that we could never find or afford on the open market. Even better, through the process of building, collecting, and restoring vestiges of the farm, we have given our house a history that it never had.

ABOVE Barns are farmyard catchalls—inside and out. Ours is loaded down with a mixture of useful tools, nostalgic signs, and castaway junk.

**Michael Vowels and
Charmayne Stratton**
LOCATION: Duvall, Washington
SIZE: 1,300 sq. ft. plus a
detached shop and garage
COST: Too much
ADVICE: Willing and able?
Don't put it off!

Dorothy, the famous little girl whisked off to the Emerald City of Oz by a tornado, speaks the very words imprinted in Michael Vowels' soul: "There's no place like home." For Mike, getting home was a ten-year odyssey fraught with hardship and tragedy—buoyed along by powerful creative forces and the staying power of real friends.

The year was 1985 and Mike had already spent nearly eighteen months of nights and weekends working on his own log home. Several years earlier he had taken the "biggest bang for your buck" log-building course you could imagine—two twelve-hour days with teacher and craftsman Skip Ellsworth. Now he had five and a half acres of fertile Washington woodland, his four-wheel-drive truck, and all the right tools. Mostly working alone, he had felled and skidded enough 12-to-

16-inch-diameter fir and hemlock trees for the walls, rafters, floor joists, and beams of his small, tall house (two and a half stories, 25-by-25 feet square). When it came time to raise the walls and structural timbers, all of Mike's buddies pitched in to help at two good old-fashioned work parties. You know you've got friends, says Mike, when one of them shows up at your party with not one but two cranes! With the shell up, Mike set to work sheathing, insulating, and tar-papering the roof. He planned to finish it with his own hand-split cedar shakes. Then, with the roofing job just underway and only a third of the shakes split, the course of Mike's life changed forever.

Mike was a snow skier, not a good one but a great one. Not long before, he had spent three years on the national freestyle circuit, competing around the country and quite often winning. He relished the sport above all other things in his life. "I knew for certain," says Mike, "that skiing was as good as it gets." Then

FAR LEFT The lush, critter-filled woods surrounding Mike and Charlie's house are not left to chance. By owning more than five acres of land, Mike was eligible to participate in the State Department of Natural Resources' incentive program that teaches management skills and good stewardship. With the basics in hand, Mike devised and implements his own forest plan in exchange for a 60-percent break on his property taxes. "Now," Charlie says, "Mike wants trees, but I want sculptures." The 1,200-pound life-size bear is just one of many surprise pieces you'll find lurking in their woods.

LEFT Ever since Mike finished a log-building course in 1973, he has scoured old job sites for usable leftovers. He collected everything from rebar and washers to the wood doors that lead into his home. His recycled front door is cloaked in sheets of etched brass. The strap-iron hardware from a catalog is just for show. If you come to visit, a hearty shake on the old cowbell door ringer will announce your arrival.

RIGHT As the house progressed, Mike says he met some of the finest craftsmen he has ever known. Ron Kennedy's spiral staircase empties into the third-floor master suite under the watchful eyes and playful antics of Dave Barnhart's chain-saw animals. Ron also crafted the geometric mountains ranging over the bed.

BELOW In the "design by committee" process that molded this home, shapes and angles were playthings. For the front elevation, triangle windows didn't work because they made the square house look like a jack-o-lantern, but squeezed into the bathroom they were perfect.

one Sunday in March, Mike lost control and slammed back-first into a tree. When he woke up in the hospital he was a T-8 paraplegic. Suddenly, Mike says, he was out of a job, finished with his dream home, and he could no longer walk. "It was as bad as it gets."

When Mike left the hospital four months later, he knew he had to get his building dried-in or risk losing everything to the elements. He organized another work party of friends, who completed the job in a record two days' time. With the house protected, the job site closed down.

In the time that followed, Mike's life evolved around grueling physical therapy, his new job as a construction manager, and a cautious relationship with Charmayne (Charlie) Stratton, a petite powerhouse who would one day be his wife. Mike had plenty to put behind him, but his log house—a major piece of unfinished business—was a constant nag. He visited the site every six months or so, but four and a half years passed before something unexpected happened.

It was April of 1989, and Mike was sitting at the house with a friend who had come to trim the weathered log ends. When the chain saw took a big pitchy bite of fir, fresh sawdust gushed out, and Mike caught that sappy fragrance of new-cut wood. The hook was set. Mike didn't see an end in sight—but the time had come to start again.

From that day on, Mike spent nearly every weekend for four and a half more years at the site along with an ever-changing crew of carpenters willing to work on what would normally be their days off. The house would not be the same. Mike's wheelchair saw to that. What started out as a simple, dirt-cheap, one-man operation became a well-supervised free-for-all. Everyone who worked on the house was openly encouraged to criticize the design, embellish it, or share new ideas. Details became important and light bulbs started going on. The long years of building afforded an unlikely combination of artisans the opportunity to unleash creative forces that left Mike and Charlie shaking their heads. A slew of quirky characters with job-site nicknames like "Land Surfer Dave" and "Clyde, Clyde, the cow's outside" would suddenly be Michelangelos when they held a chain saw or mason's trowel. One thing led to another, and Mike says, "We couldn't stop. We tricked out the whole house!"

Apart from the explosion of artistic expression, other changes and additions to Mike's original plan included a detached garage and shop built with a large expanse of accessible deck connected to the main house. He also needed an elevator if he

wanted to live on all three floors. That was tricky business, since an approved elevator was unthinkably expensive. Mike installed a battery-powered truck winch to operate his cage, then used a lot of "smoke and mirrors" to get the device by his building inspector. It was also becoming clear that he would marry Charlie, and the two of them planned room by room, designing each small space for function, accessibility—and children. (Eventually, Charlie would travel halfway around the world to adopt an infant daughter and son.)

What for Mike began as an awesome opportunity to experience building straight from the land became an epic journey to a place that is in its truest essence *home*. For Mike and Charlie their house has nothing to do with equity or resale value—nor, says Mike, is it a stepping-stone, mile marker, or showplace. This is where Mike started once, then started over. Now, he says, it is a place to appreciate and spend time with the family and friends who helped him get here.

ABOVE Cooking is one of Mike's specialties—not the everyday stuff, but the fancy kind you serve to good friends. A low, retractable work counter makes a handy food-prep station, and Mike can roll his chair right up to the sink. Most everything he needs on a regular basis is stored within reach, but high or low, every available nook and cranny is used for storage or to showcase some little treasure.

Mark and Patrice Cole
LOCATION: Hailey, Idaho
SIZE: 2,100 sq. ft.
COST: $38/sq. ft. for remodel
and addition
BUILDING TIME: 1991–1994
ADVICE: Live somewhere else
when the sawdust flies!

BELOW The addition of a pass-through library and master bedroom turned this boxy logger into an L shape. New decking provides dining and lounging space accessible from either wing. A small bit of forest was whittled away to make room for a yard, but during the backhoe's brief but necessary reign of terror, great care was taken to spare the aspen tree that grows through the deck.

In 1990, with two toddlers in tow, Patrice Cole frequently found herself driving from California to Idaho to visit her mother. "Was it me needing Mom, or Mom needing the grandkids?" She's not sure, but that tangible tug of family led her and her husband, Mark, to peruse local real estate. The house they found was a vacation cabin belonging to an Idaho potato farmer. Built with three-sided sawn logs, it was wedged into a snaggle of cottonwood and aspen trees near the river. Dated by its few meager furnishings—an orange beanbag chair in one corner, a macrame plant hanger in the other—the 1,200-square-foot cabin seemed lonely, unloved, and, adds Patrice, "cheesy."

When the "poor thing" hadn't sold by Christmas, Mark and Patrice bought it. In February, when their furniture came from the reasonably warm climes of Southern California to the bleak snow-barred doorstep of their Idaho fixer-upper, the movers offered the Coles their condolences.

Though Mark had been a manager, not a carpenter, he had waded through the entire Sunset series of how-to-build books. Through lessons learned by trial and error, he had successfully performed surgery on his former home and was eager to take on this new patient. Before the week was up, Mark and Patrice were ripping out the old to make way for the new.

The couple worked in stages so there was always a place in the house to eat, sleep, and change diapers. They took on one bathroom at a time and saved the kitchen for last.

With the approach of warmer weather, a foundation was readied for the 713-square-foot addition of a pass-through library and spacious master suite. That summer, Mark stacked those logs himself with a come-and-go contingent of arm-twisted friends. His self-sufficient prowess earned him the job-site nickname of "Pa," after that resolute dad on television reruns of *Little House on the Prairie.* ("Mark's favorite show," chimes Patrice. "He owns the whole series on video.")

Apart from the addition, a walk-in entry was added, and the living room was both brightened and enlarged by closing in a light-filching covered porch with a wall of windows. New decking was extended beyond that, while the raised back deck was replaced with a ground-level patio. That was a maintenance thing, ex-

plains Patrice. "At first we hadn't realized that as we shoveled snow from the roofs, we would have to double shovel the decks." (Eventually, Mark recast that retired redwood decking into a rustic potting shed that even Martha Stewart would approve of.)

Mark and Patrice did most of the remodeling themselves, getting help on occasion with tasks such as the rough-in plumbing and a portion of the Sheetrocking. Two years later they were ready to take on the kitchen and finish off plywood floors laid bare almost from the beginning. By then they were ready to call in local craftsmen to build kitchen cabinets and overlay plywood floors with pine.

ABOVE Log walls of the original house were carried only partway up. The top portions were framed then sided with half logs, and most of the interior walls were covered over with Sheetrock. For a shady wood-cuddled cabin like this one, clean and bright interior walls are a plus.

BELOW The potting shed, framed with recycled decking, precipitated a quest for barnwood siding that took the Coles on a journey back into Idaho's farming history. One thing led to another, and before long the couple found themselves at the kitchen table of an old-timer brimming over with tales passed down from generations before him. Now his old truck gate is their potting-shed bench, and bits and pieces of his historic farm were used for siding and trim.

RIGHT This pint-size pass-through library connects the original structure to the master-suite addition. It is really just a short double-wide section of hallway, but with large picture windows it feels cozy, not cramped.

As workmen installed the softwood floors, Patrice trailed after them with torture tools in hand. Using Mark's drill with a Dremel bit, boards poked through with nails, and their dog's chain, she roughed up the floor to soften the blow from the inevitable onslaught of her young family.

As devout aficionados of old country style, the Cole's had been seeking out a dated gas range and oven to "anchor" their kitchen. On a trip through Watts, California, they struck gold. A 1932 Magic Chef oven had just arrived at the store. Not caring to have it re-enameled, the treasure was a real "deal." The salesman was amused when the Cole's explained that "we pay extra to have things distressed in our town!"

When Mark and Patrice started their remodeling, they had an idea they might sell it one day and buy something a little nicer. No longer. The transformation is complete, and they are as much a part of their home as it is of them.

Unquestionably, the hardest part was living in the mess, but sacrifice can be endearing. And, while time erodes those memories of chaos and clutter, the value of neighboring real estate continues to climb. Updated and untangled, their cabin is already worth twice the money they have into it. Without a doubt, their patient investment of time and labor has earned them a nest ready for those proverbial eggs.

RIGHT Mark gutted the old kitchen and made it bigger by tearing out a wall on the left that had formed a cramped hallway to the laundry room and garage. Now the family accesses that area straight through the kitchen and past their 1932 Magic Chef oven—a unique country collectible that would not have fit in the original space. Gone, too, is the scuffed vinyl flooring, replaced by brick pavers laid down by Mark and Patrice. Farm-red cabinets were built by Ketchum craftsman Rich Evans.

 SECOND TIME AROUND

Face it. America is a throw-away society. We'll often buy new before we'll fix the old. We aren't maliciously wasteful, but we live in an affluent superstore culture that encourages a kind of routine extravagance not known in most other countries. The flip side of this coin is the tremendous potential we have to find and use recycled materials for our homes.

Of course, a house built with old logs may be the sum and substance of a recycled home, but it doesn't stop there. Given persistence, imagination, and an amenable attitude, you can breathe new life into almost anything you can think of. In this chapter, owner-builders have incorporated secondhand wood, doors, windows, appliances, fixtures, flooring, roofing, and more into new homes.

Turning another man's junk into veritable treasure can be economically, environmentally, and historically rewarding, but you will have to dedicate yourself to the task of finding it, sorting through it, and hauling it home. That takes time and a reverse-order kind of thinking. Your materials may actually dictate your design, not the other way around. For example, before we built our own home, we uncovered a cache of true divided-light windows and French doors. All but new, they had come off a botched project in California and were had for ten cents on the dollar. There were enough for our entire

house, but some of the exterior doors were over eight feet tall, and four of the windows were exceedingly long and narrow. In response, we raised our ceiling heights and tweaked our design to feature what we had. Our flexibility saved us around $20,000!

As a hands-on homebuilder you should also be familiar with uniform building standards and local codes. This goes double when you're dealing with dated goods that will impact the structural integrity or safety of your house. Wood must be sound, weight-bearing members need to meet certain standards, bedroom windows must be large enough to provide emergency exits, stairways shouldn't be too steep, and so on.

You will also want to consider energy efficiency and function when hauling home items such as old windows, appliances, and fixtures. Then, if it breaks, can somebody fix it? Let your common sense prevail, and keep your family's health and well-being in mind, particularly when you outfit your home with older heating systems or electrical devices.

Having meted out obligatory words of caution, we encourage you to try something old if it meets your needs and fits your budget. Replace that "new is better" attitude from the start, and prepare yourself for a trip that you may enjoy as much as your destination.

Steve and Cecilia Abbey
LOCATION: Bellevue, Idaho
SIZE: 1,600 sq. ft.
COST: $56,000 ($35/sq. ft.)
BUILDING TIME: 1995–1996
ADVICE: Ask the experts, but
set a budget, prioritize,
and prepare to compromise.

When Steve Abbey was growing up, his father was a diplomatic major general in the air force. Much of his youth was spent in Europe where his dad worked, and his mom collected antiques with a passion. Steve grins when he recalls his last day in Holland. He was a teenager, and his family was preparing to leave the country on a ship bound for America. "While we were boarding, my mom was still hunting down treasures at the flea market. She damned near missed the boat!" Steve, however, a collector following in his mother's footsteps, certainly did not.

ABOVE Antiquated wood and century-old posts frame the newest section of the Abbeys' three-part house. To meet code, Steve spent about $300 per cabin beefing up original tin roofs that had already weathered nearly 120 years in the valley. The front door is solid hand-carved walnut, and once hailed access to the music hall in a European castle.

Steve and his wife, Cecilia, are collectors extraordinaire. Buying, trading, and selling is done with such entrepreneurial flair that they have built a home valued at more than $150 per square foot for about a quarter of the price. Steve has an eye for value and knows that if he buys recycled goods in quantity, he can keep what he needs and sell the rest at a profit. He's done this over and over again, amassing wood, doors, cabinets, kitchen appliances, and even the lot he built on. He has a comparable strategy when it comes time to finding help. He keeps tabs on construction sites in the valley, and when building slows down, he offers off-time laborers work at a reduced rate. Instead of paying $18 or $20 an hour, he may pay $12 or less to people who would rather keep busy than sit home unemployed.

None of this makes sense, says Steve, if you're in a hurry or paying interest on a big bank loan. When you are building with recycled materials, it takes time—

FAR RIGHT The living room is the central framed section of the house and shares log walls with bookend cabins. Other walls are Sheetrocked inside and covered with recycled shiplap siding. In the hall beyond the living room, wainscoting and oak molding once lined the interior of an 1890 apothecary shop.

RIGHT In its day this green door opened and closed on a lot of living. Now, knobs and hinges stand idle on an entryway that the Abbeys reserve for unsolicited visitors. If it actually opened, you would find yourself nose to nose with the back of a gasburning Heartland stove in their kitchen.

Steve figures at least two years of stockpiling just to get you started. Auctions, the classifieds, garage sales, remodels, and jobsite dumpsters are good places to begin. Watch for old buildings slated for razing or fire department training burns. When Steve was finally ready to go, he recalls, "I had fifteen different piles of wood stacked up under cover in my yard. It was like building from an Erector set!"

The body of the Abbey house is defined by two 1882 log cabins flanking a central stick-built section. One of them, a small single-story fashioned from cottonwood and aspen trees, had been completely reclothed in Victorian garb in 1890. Not a log was visible. Its present-day owner would have bulldozed it, but Steve got there first and claimed the doomed house in exchange for moving it and cleaning up the site. Covered over with sound shiplap siding and filled with beaded-board paneling and other usable wood, it was a valuable find.

The second home was a two-story cabin built of Douglas fir and stuffed with newspaper insulation dating back to 1881. Steve imagines that settlers moving west in covered wagons brought the paper wrapped around precious dishes and other household goods. Unlike the East, finding cabins so old in Idaho is uncommon, since most were hastily built and eventually burned down or were ravaged by the harsh ruse of nature.

Steve didn't want to dismantle either building, since he was convinced they would never go back together as tightly as they'd been put up. Instead, he crossbraced doors and windows, then stiffened walls by screwing 2-by-6 boards vertically onto the log ends at each corner. Individually, the cabins were jacked up, loaded onto

ABOVE When Tyson chicken farms replaced 150,000 wooden coops with sanitary metal boxes, they were doing the poultry business a favor. But when they burned the old coops, they brought tears to the eyes of many a collector. Now, the one displaying Cecilia's china cows might fetch $300 in an antique store. Stained glass in the kitchen and living room color in window openings left from the original cabin.

LEFT Beaded-board paneling in the kitchen was salvaged from one of the 1882 log cabins. Under-counter cabinets and most of the appliances came from a multimillion-dollar house undergoing remodeling nearby. Steve bought the whole kitchen, kept what he needed, then sold the rest. In the white hutch purchased from Pancho Villa's niece, blue and white Abbey china mingle with fine Delft china from Holland. Though the namesake is only coincidental, Steve's family has collected the Abbey line for three generations.

BELOW When Steve moved and washed the cabins, most of the loose mud and concrete chink fell out. Re-chinking was a messy, time-consuming task. Steve and Cecilia resealed the logs in the kitchen and bedroom but didn't bother with the living room since there was no need to insulate those walls from the weather.

a flatbed, and delivered to his neighborhood lot. The log homes were reset on opposite ends of a pre-readied foundation. Their roof lines were left intact and the stick-built section of the house was pieced in between.

Both structures were a mess when they arrived. The two-story cabin had been lived in up until 1929, then was demoted to a barn for cows. The rotting, bottom two courses of logs had to be replaced on each building. Steve swapped the bad wood with trees of the same species that he'd carefully shaped and hewed to match. Siding inside and out was removed along with buckets of square nails. It took a week just to yank the nails in a single room! The logs were blasted with 1,000 psi of water to clean them up and restore some of their original color. Finally, log oil was applied inside and out.

Every window and door opening in the two early homesteads was left almost as it had been found. No new holes were added, and none were walled in. Because custom windows are outrageously expensive, Steve padded some of the openings to fit recycled windows he had on hand. For proper ventilation he utilized operable windows on north and south exposures, but incorporated less-expensive fixed glass on the east and west sides.

The Abbeys are quality conscious but don't believe you always need the best of everything. Sometimes, explains Steve, it's just plain overkill. When you're on a budget, you should talk with the experts to find out what's available and how things are done. Then you make decisions based on where you want to spend your money. In undertaking a project like his, Steve says it helps to have some building experience—particularly when you're rooting around for core supplies. If you know what you'll need throughout the process, you're less likely to pass up usable scrap. But, says Steve, you can get by without it—if you have the time, that is, and know how to take advantage of the knowledge of others.

Bob and Marti's reverence for old-world craftsmanship and the Adirondack legacy is evident in the finishing touches. Working alongside local artisans Jim Stoddard and Rick Buffum, the couple made liberal use of bentwood and recycled cedar posts. Reminiscent of old Appalachia, the porch sits up on piles of back-jointed, "almost" dry-stacked rocks, while the cabin's concrete block foundation and chimney are faced with stone laid up in the same way.

Bob and Marti Fulton
Kwana-Ci Lodge
LOCATION: Westcliffe, Colorado
SIZE: 1,315 sq. ft.
COST: $100/sq. ft.
BUILDING TIME: 1996
ADVICE: Patience, patience!

A chilly wind sent new-fallen leaves skipping over headstones in the little mountain cemetery. With hands thrust deep in our pockets, we wondered out loud about the stealing sickness that had taken one family's three small children just days apart nearly a century ago. As we moved on, a new curiosity caught Marti's eye. Stooping to the ground, she dug free a worn metal hook. That familiar smile crept into her eyes as she shared the find with her husband, Bob. Really, it was just what they'd been looking for!

Bob and Marti Fulton were always on the prowl for something—anything—

they could work into their Appalachian-style cabin. Recycled from old barns, moonshiners' shanties, chicken coops, and a hundred other forgotten scrap piles, the Fulton's 1,300-square-foot home is a combination of history and art. Bob and Marti have done much of the work themselves, but the handiwork of local craftsmen adds something unexpected.

In the fall of 1995 the couple had looked at prepackaged log homes and were less than a week away from placing an order when a newspaper ad for old beams landed on the breakfast table. The wood was part of a condemned warehouse still standing in Denver. Bob drove to the site, took one look, and bought them on the spot. Marti was horrified. Maybe the

LEFT The Fultons' arrival in Westcliffe signaled amnesty for piles of ancient barn wood destined for bonfires at half a dozen valley ranches. Hand-made doors, porch and window trim, and interior wood walls all glory in their born-again silver patina.

BELOW Collecting requires a sharp eye, perseverance, and hard work, but knowing what to do with the stuff you find is an art. Bob and Marti often haul stuff home, then figure out what to do with it later. For instance, this dormer is sheathed in rusted corrugated metal and lit up with a fixture devised from the grill of a 1930s truck. On the ceiling the Fultons installed formed-plastic replicas of patterned tin from Snellings Thermo Vac.

kit house wasn't exactly what she'd had in mind, but then, neither could she imagine these charred, paint-flecked, bee-ridden logs as walls in their house. Marti didn't know then that Bob had already re-hewed each beam in his mind. It would only be a matter of time before he'd adze them clean all over again at their building site.

Relying on Charles McRaven's book *Building the Hewn Log House* and a borrowed *This Old House* video, Bob and crew member Perry Dunlap taught themselves to cut dovetail notches and put them together. Bob believes that if something can

be taught, he can learn it. He and Marti designed the cabin themselves using common sense, an awareness of snow loads, and something they call the "massive attitude." If a 1-by-2 would work, they would beef up construction with a 2-by-3 or 2-by-4 instead.

Bob approaches building with the contagious enthusiasm of a child at Christmas. The scent of old wood sends Bob careening down less-traveled roads and knocking on strangers' doors. With Bob, though, no one stays a stranger for long. When construction started, he moved into the Westcliffe Bed and Breakfast. While Marti tended to their horses and a house that hadn't sold back in Golden, Colorado, Bob held court with the locals each morning over coffee. Before long, he knew everyone in town, where they lived, and the year and make of their trucks.

Now he regularly visits the ranching families in the valley and wanders through their tilting sheds and abandoned coops. His new friends are genuinely amused at his penchant for stuff they can't wait to get rid of. Sometimes the Fultons have relied on other dealers to help them find things such as period light fixtures or wide pine flooring. Other times, they couldn't find "old" at all and were forced to buy new.

RIGHT This exceptional stairway was literally an after-thought. The ridge beam and rafters were in place when Bob decided to use an entire tree inside his house. He and a small crew trekked twenty miles to find this ponderosa pine. It was still living when they topped it and hauled it back. After the debarking process, a torch was used to char the trunk, then it was sanded and finished with two coats of beeswax and gum turpentine. Rafters were removed and a crane employed to drop the tree into place. Scrub oak and antlers were crafted into railings.

PHOTOGRAPH BY LARRY SIMMONS

ABOVE Antler-handled French doors open from the master bedroom to the living room, where a propane-fired stove is flued into the outside chimney through a decorative sheet of old tin above the mantel. Around Bob's dry-stacked fireplace, drama unfolds in the scene carved by Jim Stoddard. Still in the works, it will eventually include a waterfall cascading down the tin into a pool around the fish.

As the cabin progressed, the Fultons hired local craftsmen to help with the finish work. "We had no grand plan," says Bob. "We made decisions as we went and changed things every day." Caught up in the art and excitement of building, the crew worked at a frenzied pace, executing new ideas and throwing barn wood up everywhere. "At first we got ahead of ourselves," says Bob. When they finally found their rhythm, craftsmanship slowed down flying fingers, and the Fultons found some of their work had to be redone. But the work overall was amazing, and creativity exploded like kernels of sizzling corn. Bob fashioned light fixtures out of old truck parts, mason jars, and moose antlers. His artisan crew turned logs, posts, and beams into sculpture. A spiral staircase emerged from the trunk of an entire tree. Marti, herself an artist, painted a view from a nonexistent window above the kitchen sink and added her own unique touch to cabinets, floors, and walls.

Marti told Bob that as soon as they had a place to keep their horses on the property, she would come to the cabin to stay. She forgot to include things like heat, water, and a working kitchen in the deal, and she jokes that they had plenty of nice, old manger chew boards but no place to hang toilet paper! Bob was so caught up in the artistry of the place that he didn't get around to the necessities for awhile. Then guests started coming 'round. At the Fultons', friends are always welcome, and Marti says that with each new arrival came a longed-for amenity. Now Bob has become a regular tour guide—a task he relishes with much the same enthusiasm he possessed while building this mountain masterpiece.

ABOVE Kitchen cabinets were purchased at a tent sale for ten cents on the dollar. Marti painted and antiqued them, and Jim Stoddard added decorative twig panels. Above the kitchen sink, a faux window glimpses the view over Grape Creek to the inspiring Sangre de Cristo Mountains behind the cabin. Marti will eventually paint interchangeable spring, winter, and fall views of this same scene. Aspen strips salvaged from the ash heap are used for trim.

BELOW Sweeping steep-pitched roofs, dormers, and patterned shutters give the Kennedy cabin that "come on in" feeling. Garden paths paved with salvaged ornamental bricks and sidewalk fragments lead through and around a hickory-lathe fence, hand-split before the Civil War.

Sit down with Clyde Kennedy and you'll meet a guy who's done lots of living. Born in 1923, he grew up through the Great Depression, textured by a salty clan of relations that he remembers over coffee in cry-and-laugh-out-loud stories. At the age of ten, Clyde Kennedy and his brothers already had a fix on hard work, but when they snuck off to the woods with a Zane Grey novel and their dad's crosscut saw to build their own log blockhouse, they were after imaginary Indians. What they got (besides a pint-sized cabin) were irate parents and a good dusting of leather for cutting down so many locust trees!

Clyde doesn't make a fuss over a lifetime spent getting far on little, but he has. A $300 do-it-yourself garage launched

Clyde and Dawn Kennedy
LOCATION: Rushville, Ohio
SIZE: 2,200 sq. ft.
COST: Spread over twenty years, who knows?
BUILDING TIME: 1977–1990
ADVICE: When you find a cabin hidden under old siding, don't get stuck with a pig in a poke.

LEFT Slate roofs took off in this country around 1880 and were popular until composition shingles upstaged them about thirty years later. Most of the Kennedys' slates came off the roof of a barn and old house built in 1904. Clyde reshaped them with an $8 slate cutter purchased at an auction, then put in new nail holes with a foot-operated puncher. His stairway is built with turn-of-the-century sandstone, and the light fixtures are rigged up out of old mason jars with rust-proof zinc lids.

RIGHT There is still a lot of kid left in Clyde, and he couldn't resist building a house with secret nooks, trapdoors, and gun ports—like the one under the coatrack in this main-floor kitchen. He has "all approaches covered." There are fourteen ports around the house built into chinking between the logs. Most of the time, they are open for ventilation, and copper screening keeps the bugs outside. When the weather kicks up, Clyde stuffs in handmade wooden plugs.

FAR RIGHT Diamond-patterned shutters came out of the Globe Hotel built in Bellaire, Ohio, around 1890. For years, trains had chugged by on a bridge over the hotel, and when the Kennedys bought their eight shutters for $100, they were so caked with black grit and grime that it took Clyde forty hours to restore a single pair. Now the colorful shutters are fixed to double-hung windows built from scratch out of old doors. He got his kitchen sink out of the Globe, too. Coincidentally, it is the same sink that his mother, at the age of eleven, washed dishes in while working for the hotel in 1904.

him into a satisfying building career, and a $34 wedding with a hot-dog reception landed him a bride who's stuck by him for more than fifty years. Recycling old materials and dump-bound junk into a new house just came naturally. He says, "I didn't go to the lumberyard for the wood that's in a one-foot ruler!"

Instead, the materials used in the Kennedy cabin represent years worth of haggling and poking around. Clyde never passed a demolition work site without stopping by to make friends with the foreman and to wonder casually what they were gonna do with all that scrap. It didn't matter if they were taking down an old bridge, pulling up railroad ties, remodeling a church, or knocking down a cabin—he would be there.

Clyde retired back in the seventies, and he and his wife, Dawn, broke ground on a $2,000 chunk of hilly land near West Rushville (population 200). Since a set of

building plans was not required, they worked from scaled sketches. Clyde relied on past experience, common sense, and his "If it looks good, it is good!" philosophy that sometimes set him and Dawn at loggerheads. Yielding to compromise, advises Clyde, is what keeps a marriage mellow.

Their three-story home is pieced together with the dovetailed logs from an early 1800s cabin and two old barns. The cabin and the barns were free for the taking, and the Kennedys dismantled them all by themselves. They had help with the hauling but, all told, spent less than $500. Clyde is quick to tell you that "there's a big difference between tearing something down and taking it down." He will also remind you that most of that wood lasted as long as it did because it was covered over with weatherboarding, lath, and plaster. The downside to that is he had to re-hew the inside of all those logs by hand, and that's a job he wouldn't wish on his worst enemy.

BELOW The modern maintenance-free window in the upstairs bedroom is dressed out in old wood and crowned with stained glass from a broken church window. Clyde carved the "home sweet home" sign in 1937.

The story-and-a-half cabin sits on top of an easy access daylight basement that can be ventilated in summer just by opening a door. The foundation walls below grade are built with concrete blocks salvaged from a small house. Above ground level, Clyde used solid sandstone recycled from a massive nineteenth-century Victorian chimney. The basement floor combines four-inch-thick dairy brick from Somerset, Ohio, and two-inch-thick sandstone from sidewalks laid in Rushville around the turn of the century. Most of it was free for the hauling.

Clyde and Dawn are in their seventies now and still plenty spry, but while they were sketching out their floor plan, Clyde's eighty-year-old uncle came out to help and visit. He took a quick look at the three-tiered plan and said "Think wheelchair, Clyde."

"Now, I'm not one to argue with an old guy," says Clyde, so they put their tub on the main floor even though they sleep upstairs. When the time comes, the study next to that master bath will be converted to their bedroom, and they will save the upstairs for guests.

Clyde will tell you that he learned most of what he knows about recycling and building by "hanging around older people." He recalls the summer he worked for an octogenarian who owned his own mill and lumber yard. The old guy never wasted a scrap of reject lumber and eventually filled up an entire building with odds and ends. Clyde got hired to turn those piles into a house, and his elderly employer showed him how to mix and match siding, straighten studs, and trim up corners. There wasn't a piece of siding on that building over six feet long, and Clyde says the house looked best if you

LEFT You won't find many wood sheds like this one, hand-stacked board by board. Clyde says it's really just a pile of firewood. The roof is supported on board piers so the couple can pull wood from the walls without caving in the whole shed.

viewed just one wall at a time. But he figures that he was fortunate to have that job, and has been using what he learned and adding to it ever since.

Though their bent is toward hard work, "we aren't nuts," says Clyde. As they get older, ease and efficiency are on their minds. Until 1974, the Kennedy cabin was heated with a homemade wood-burning stove retrofitted with a water jacket. As the water got hot, it expanded and circulated throughout the house to recycled cast-iron radiators. The system was simple but had Clyde out chopping five cords of wood a year to keep them warm. Now he has installed a high-efficiency, gas-fired hot-water boiler, and has traded in his ax for an oil can—five drops every six months is all it needs.

Deep well water is pumped into a buried tank up on the hills, and their drinking water comes down to the cabin by gravity. Everything else is supplied by cisterns. A submersible pump sends the rainwater into a pressure tank inside the house. Ohio averages around thirty-eight inches of rainfall a year, so they rarely get low on soft water. "But sometimes," says Clyde, "if it doesn't rain for a month, we go on yellow alert and bail the bathwater to flush the toilets. If it gets worse, we go on red alert and head for an outhouse hauled in as salvage." That hasn't happened yet.

More than twenty years have gone into the building of the Kennedys' cabin, detached garage, shop, shed, and gardens. Clyde's father always told him, "It's better to wear out than to rust out," so, as long as he's able, you won't find him sitting around. And when eventually he and Dawn do wear out they won't be going far. They have plots across the street in the old country graveyard and have every intention of "riding herd on their place until Jesus comes."

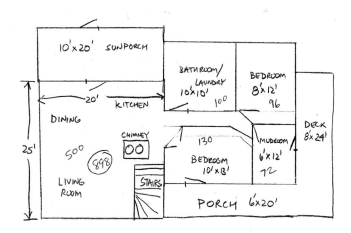

FIRST FLOOR

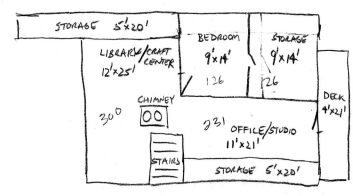

SECOND FLOOR

**Todd Gladfelter and
Cindy Ross family**
LOCATION: Near Hawk Mountain,
Pennsylvania
SIZE: 2,500 sq. ft.
COST: $20,000 ($8/sq. ft.)
BUILDING TIME: 1984–1988
ADVICE: Working together as
a couple can draw you closer.
Let that interdependence enhance
your building experience.

There are thousands of miles of hiking trails that crisscross America. The 2,100-mile Appalachian Trail, 2,600-mile Pacific Crest Trail, and 3,100-mile Continental Divide Trail are the three longest. Hiking just one in a lifetime would be a momentous exploit for most anyone, but Cindy Ross and her husband, Todd Gladfelter, have nearly hiked them all. Between the two of them, they have chalked up 18,000 miles, and by the ages of six and eight their two children had put in 2,000 and 2,500 miles respectively—mostly via the backs of llamas. Since summer always finds the family hoisting packs and wearing down boot tread, they lead an independent lifestyle that long ago defied reliance on weekly paychecks or an obligation to a mortgage.

Wholly self-reliant and energized by the challenge of doing, Cindy and Todd took their ambitious dreams of home ownership

LEFT Ever since Cindy first read Thoreau in the tenth grade, she had planned on building a log cabin in the woods. She didn't know when that would be until she met Todd, who shared her passion. They acquired their first load of logs even before they were married or owned land. The cabin quickly evolved into a home tucked away on twelve acres where they keep pack llamas, grow their own vegetables, and home-school their children.

to the Great Lakes School of Logbuilding in Ely, Minnesota. The ten-day workshop set them on a four-year course—culminating in a 2,500-square-foot house built out of pocket for $20,000. They did virtually all the work themselves, puzzling through the intricacies of each unfamiliar task, supplemented only by advice from numerous books and friends in the trade.

Working with logs selected for the proper width, height, and taper, the couple used the chinkless Swedish-scribe method of building. In the beginning, says Todd, it took them all day to pull a small six-teen-foot log out of the pile. But a few tricks later, along with the help of everything from come-alongs and boat winches to levers, block and tackle, carts, and derricks, he was maneuvering twenty-five-footers all by himself. Outside of logs, most of the wood and building materials were salvaged, including slate for their roof that was retrieved during the demolition of a nearby hospital.

Finding recycled materials was not all that difficult, says Cindy. Once you start to network and let people know you're looking, calls start coming to you.

FAR LEFT Tiles on the kitchen floor are seconds bought directly from the factory. Although the company typically sells its "B" grade merchandise to wholesalers, they said "yes" to Cindy and Todd, who shaved more than a third off the regular price. Kitchen shelves and cabinets were fashioned from leftover wood flooring, and the furniture is a mixed bag. Some pieces were carefully handcrafted by Todd, while others were plucked off of curbsides.

LEFT There's no telling how many pots of chicken and dumplings simmered on top of Cindy and Todd's large coal- and wood-burning stove before it arrived in their kitchen. They continue to use it for both cooking and heating, but it is not the sole source for either. The firebox is too small to heat the entire house in the dead of winter, so a second no-nonsense wood burner is flued into the brick chase around the corner.

Contractors and carpenters are a great resource. One of their builder friends told them about an ill-fated pole barn "as big as a ball field." Wood trusses hadn't held and the whole thing collapsed. The insurance company was going to burn it, but the word went out that anything carted off first would be for the keeping. The Gladfelters hauled home "tons of lumber"!

ABOVE As a furniture maker, Todd enjoyed creating doors with different themes and designs. After the couple finished the main house, they salvaged logs from a small hewn barn. Todd turned those logs into a 250-square-foot cabin for his wife to write in. With the structure nearly finished, Todd banished Cindy from his shop, then surprised her with this personalized screen door.

Alley shopping has also yielded its share of booty. Driving through the dumpster-laden byways of Hamburg one evening, Cindy and Todd happened across twenty-four windows slated for the trash. While they were not the most energy-efficient, the couple used the majority in a sunroom that gets closed off from the main house during prolonged bouts of harsh weather. Other nonoperable windows in the home were fixed into openings with an extra pane or two of glass. For ventilation, six-inch spaces were cut below each one, then sealed with a chunk of thick, removable foam.

Cindy makes her living writing experience-based outdoor travel books and articles, while Todd is a fine furniture builder. He knows how to wield a hammer and saw, says Cindy, but he's no plumber or electrician. Today, the thought of taking on such tasks would scare most people away. The fact is, that's how houses got built years ago, and despite what the experts tell you, it can still be done. Keep your design simple, advises Cindy, and you'll find that once you conquer a task, it will empower you. One skill builds on the next, she says, and your level of confidence climbs right along with it.

They admit there were a few glitches and the work was stressful at times. The slate roof was particularly tough. Framing contractors didn't have the answers they needed, and their log-building teacher could only be reached by radio-phone. That meant the Gladfelters were on their own for the most part. In the end,

they basically built two roofs. They started with log trusses and purlins. Then, concerned with the weight of the slate (3,000 tiles weighing more than ten tons), they supplemented with a system of rafters.

Witnessing the couple sacrifice and struggle over the years, incredulous family members wondered if it was really worth it. For seven years before building the house, Cindy and Todd had worked as volunteers in the national parks program, running a hostel for long-distance hikers. They had lived mostly rent-free in a tiny park-service cabin on the side of Hawk Mountain near the Appalachian Trail. There was no plumbing, and in winter the dark, poorly insulated space was so cold that Cindy's pee bucket would freeze solid in the night. But Todd figures that the rent they saved over those seven years—conservatively, maybe $300 a month—would have added up to about $20,000. And that, he says, is exactly what they have put into this house!

Now the couple figures they make around $20,000 a year. They put $5,000 into savings and $6,000 goes for insurance and taxes. That doesn't leave a lot, but it is enough to feed a hiking habit that has gained them international recognition through acquaintances and the books Cindy writes. In May of 1996, a nonprofit hiking group in the Czech Republic invited the entire family to christen a newly constructed 250-mile greenway from Vienna, Austria, to Prague. The couple consulted with the group, helping them develop the recreation potential for the

hiking, biking, and horseback-riding trail that connects cultural monuments, ancient communities, castles, and churches along the way.

At this writing, Todd and Cindy were hiking 3,100 miles with their children, Bryce and Sierra, along the continental divide from Canada to Mexico. They travel 500 miles at a stretch and began the journey when the kids were just one and three years old. The family's llamas have saddled Bryce and Sierra for much of the way, but when the journey ends, the last 900 miles will have been covered on tandem mountain bikes. Cindy's next book will retell their adventures and celebrate a deliberate choice of lifestyle that, for them, has made their carefree travels possible—and yes, definitely worth it!

ABOVE At log-building school the teacher advised everyone to build a practice cabin first. Cindy recalls how "our class would bust their butts working logs all day, then at night we'd relax together in the sauna. We got to be like family." It was such a good experience and delicious way to unwind that the couple chose to "practice" on a sauna of their own.

BELOW This, says one British friend, is "the loo with a view." Following the instructions of the Gunnison County Building Department, the privy sits atop a culvert eight feet deep. The bottom is sealed with cement, and, given enough use, will need pumping. The giant signature tire is functional art—keeping vehicles from pulling too far forward into the yard.

Frank and Mary Vader
LOCATION: Taylor Reservoir, Colorado
SIZE: 900 sq. ft.
COST: $10,000 ($11/sq. ft.)
BUILDING TIME: 1990–1991
ADVICE: An effective house-raising is a well-organized event where tools and materials are on hand, and tasks are broken down and well-defined.

Some people will incorporate just about anything into the landscape of their home. And while it has been said that necessity is the mother of invention, Frank Vader would have to add that his commitment to recycling a particularly persistent form of rubbish and the availability of that material also figured heavily into his low-budget approach to site prep. Though Frank and his family built their $10,000 cabin retreat with dead-standing logs, Frank collected more than 500 old tires to shore up the hillside behind his home and line his driveway. Why tires? "Well, they're free," says Frank, but he's also bothered by the fact that those things just fill up the dumps. Once you bury them, they don't rot, and he hates that kind of waste.

Planning ahead, Frank accumulated spent tires from a couple of local shops

over a two-year period. Normally it wouldn't take that long, but he wanted them all to be the same size. He squirreled away other useful items too—like recycled building supplies, yard-sale furniture, a wood-burning stove, and doors salvaged from a meat locker.

When Frank was ready to build, he hired a tractor to carve a level building pad into the hillside on the family's two-acre lot. He and his friends eventually packed all 500 tires with soil and worked them into the retaining walls around the house and down the driveway. It was a labor-intensive way to go. They had to shovel and tamp a lot of dirt, and that

dirt needed to be moist. Since water hadn't made it to the site, they put the spring season to task by using water-soaked earth. It took them two years, working primarily through the months of May to finish the job.

While the hillside was bedecked with tires, a cellar was dug back into it. Frank scraped out a 6-by-16-foot room, then lined it with more free tread and foam insulation recovered from a remodel. He built a heavy door out of rough-cut planks and added a padlock. Now he had a frost-free place to store his tools, miscellaneous supplies, and canned goods. Next, Frank and Mary constructed

ABOVE Perched on a silent hill in the company of clouds and shifting shadows, the Vaders' cabin is surrounded on three sides by National Forest Service land. In the wintertime the snowplow stops four miles back at the Taylor Park Trading Post, and Frank will often ski in alone. The cabin is sheathed with strong barn metal that shines like a beacon. Frank's old boss says, "It goes on ugly and never changes," but Frank says it is practical and won't fade like colored metal.

a fine-looking post-and-beam log outhouse. When comfortably seated inside, you are drenched with light and treated to a restful view through the wall built entirely of glass.

The 900-square-foot cabin is framed with 8-by-8 posts and beams, then in-filled with logs. Working in the fall, Frank logged his wood off an old burn in Taylor Park, then hauled it back to his shop. During the winter, in the protection of his well-tooled work space, he milled posts and beams and pre-notched them with mortise-and-tenon joints. Logs for the walls were squared off on two sides and the window bucks pre-cut. In the summers, he was too busy overseeing operations on his employer's ranch to do much building, so it wasn't until the following fall that he returned to his site to lay the foundation and erect the prefabricated skeletal framework of the cabin.

With the prep work done, he and Mary arranged a house-raising and chili feed that brought fifty eager friends out in blustery October weather. Frank spent most of the day supervising well-organized groups of red-cheeked volunteers. Almost everyone had some building experience in one area or another. Frank assigned tasks accordingly, leaving no one out. One crew tackled the well and pump, one the walls, another the staircase.

A few loyal friends stayed through the week to help finish off the roof and install the windows. There is no electricity or indoor plumbing, so nothing was

too complicated, says Frank. Actually, he says, it all went far better than he even imagined, and he feels real good about involving so many of his friends and neighbors. Having spent his whole life in Gunnison County, Frank appreciates the strong sense of camaraderie among the people he works with and lives near. They wanted to pitch in, and involving them literally left the door open to enhanced relationships. All the Vaders' friends who helped on the cabin have some limited access to the place. "It's one of the perks," says Frank. Most often his friends visit in the summer to fish in the icy waters of the Taylor Park Reservoir just half a mile away. His own family gets more use in the winter, when Frank's work lets up a little. They may sled or ski some, but mostly it's their place to relax.

RIGHT Frank jokes that if you want running water at their cabin, you fill your bucket from the hand pump then run to the house. The kitchen sink is the only place to wash up, and gray water drains into a pit outside.

FAR RIGHT At breakfast time the cry goes out for good hot coffee and homemade beer biscuits warm from the cookstove and dripping with honey. This fine old stove passed down from Mary's family has never failed them. Without electricity, gas-powered lights and wood heat are comforting and reliable. Like much of the woodwork and some of the furniture, the kitchen cupboards were prefabricated in Frank's shop. The metal cabinet faces were salvaged from a meat locker.

Steven and Jaimie Anne Stegman
LOCATION: Otego, New York
SIZE: 1,896 sq. ft., including
a 436-sq.-ft. cellar
COST: $40,000 ($21/sq. ft.)
BUILDING TIME: 1980s, five years
ADVICE: Read up!

Steven Stegman was barely twenty-two years old but knew what he wanted. Two years earlier he had put together a small model of the log home he intended to build on land he expected to own. He wasn't sure where exactly that would be, but he had it all worked out on paper. He wanted about ten acres accessed by a maintained road, yet well out of town. He needed both hardwood and softwood trees, along with water for a stream or pond. Not really ready to buy, he gave his list to a realtor, "mostly just to practice shopping." But when the agent called back a week later and took him to the perfect spot, it was suddenly time to practice buying. The seller had forty acres and was asking $500 apiece. Steven didn't

have it, but he didn't have anything to lose either, so he offered less than half. When his offer was accepted, the time had come to practice building!

In the beginning, Steven had a little construction experience, had a lot of ski-ing experience, and could ride a mule bareback. As it turns out, the time spent hanging on to that mule paid off first. Steven planned to horse-log his property and bought himself a giant Clydesdale named Spot. Spot had plenty of giddy-up but was too darn big for a saddle. When Steven discovered (quite unexpect-edly) that Spot could jump over minor obstacles like stone walls, it was the mule he remembered in his prayers that night.

Working on and off through three seasons, man and horse cleared the land. Steven built a makeshift log barn for the two of them to live in. Winters were still spent ski instructing in Taos, New Mexico, so this was phase one of a project that would take years to complete. Steven says Spot was a faithful coworker but made a lousy roommate. Thus came a second building that man (not beast) would live in—a small, unplumbed, part log/part frame cabin that would later be converted into a sauna and playhouse for visiting friends.

Things were done bit by bit as time and money allowed. Initially, Steven didn't have any power to his site, but he really didn't need any. He squared up tamarack logs with an Alaskan chain-saw mill—a slow and awkward device utilizing a regular chain saw as the cutting tool. (Not recommended, says Steven, unless you

FAR LEFT Garden-grown pumpkins salute autumn from the Stegmans' welcoming front porch. The stairs are built with rocks from an old foundation discovered on the property, and slabs for the treads were cut from a local quarry. Steven's log shell settled for over two years. When he got around to the finish work, flexible synthetic chinking, though impressive, had too many zeros on the price tag. That left good old-fashioned mortar instead.

RIGHT Steven finished off his floors, cabinets, stairs, and trim with a medley of different wood species nearly all logged on his property. Oak, cherry, and maple are just a few. Because the wood still shrinks and swells slightly with the seasons, the kitchen cabinets get harder to close in the summer and harder to keep closed in the winter!

FAR RIGHT Power didn't make it to the house until 1989—shortly after a thief broke into the Stegmans' cellar and stole their generator. According to Steven, that old piece of junk wouldn't have made a good ship's anchor, but their insurance company came through with replacement value, so they used the money to bring in electricity. That's when the finish work really got underway. The rock fireplace is detailed with chestnut beams and oak braces salvaged from a barn down the road. Friends call Steven the "Ax Man," and the door handle is his personal signature.

have your whole life to saw wood. Eventually he cried uncle and sent some of his logs to a local mill). He notched each log end into a classic dovetail and single-handedly jockeyed them into place.

Nearly all the core building materials came off the land or were salvaged from various sources nearby. The stones in the massive two-story, triple-flued fireplace came from the crumbling foundation of an original homestead on his property. The fireplace, with Steven's own custom-built, cast-iron doors, is the very heart of his home and the source of his innovative heating system. His large firebox is cloaked in a hollow steel jacket that holds water warmed by the fire. The heated liquid is transferred to a 500-gallon, stainless-steel storage tank in the cellar, then moved by a series of pumps to hydronic radiant and baseboard heaters throughout the house. Steven lined the fireplace with his own soapstone cement. Although the solid soapstone slabs quarried in nearby Vermont were not in his budget, piles of residual soapstone filings were free. Steven bagged the stuff, trucked it home, and turned it into bricks. Soapstone is known for superior heat-retention properties, and he says his jury-rigged offspring performs surprisingly well.

It takes almost two days to get the water warm enough to heat the house, but once the system is ready, the rooms will stay toasty for three days without a fire.

ABOVE A window-side chair in the master bedroom is a quiet place to view the woods and watch the seasons change. Jaimie painted the radiant baseboard heaters to blend in with the logs.

RIGHT The deck overlooking the garden and two-acre pond was the latest addition to the Stegman home. Like so many ongoing house projects, Jaimie said they had talked about it, drawn pictures of it, and lived with the image in their minds for so many years that when it finally arrived, it was as if it had always been there.

Each year, twelve to fifteen cords of wood are cut to fuel the system, but there is no shortage of that on Steven's property. In the case of an extended trip away from home, a backup gas-powered hot-water boiler kicks in.

Having water on the property provided Steven with the opportunity to configure a system of ponds and a small stream where "pet fish grow as big as your leg!" His house overlooks the largest body of water—a two-acre pond that he dredged out with the help of a rented backhoe. His little cabin-turned-sauna sits on the bank of a smaller pond surrounded by tall trees, decked out with a diving platform and rope swings. Around 1985 Steven met his future wife, Jamie, in New Mexico and brought her back to his evolving homestead. When they were sitting outside one evening, choirs of frogs began to perform. Starting in one pond and moving up the valley, frogs belted out in succession while working up to a powerful crescendo. Such a choreographed production has never been repeated, but that peculiar show of singing amphibians inspired the Stegmans to dub their back forty Frog Hollow.

When Steven started his project nearly twenty years ago friends told him he was crazy. Today some of those same people are still paying off thirty-year mortgages, while Steve just paid as he went. He was able to develop his property in a way that got the most out of the site, and the friends who come to visit now don't want to leave.

4 HANDMADE ORIGINALS

ABOVE Early *cabins* were not homes. They were temporary shelters built hastily with round logs. Most did not endure. A *home,* on the other hand, was carefully constructed with logs hewn smooth and flat. This 1869 dwelling is a bit of both. The logs were left round outside but were properly adzed on the interior. It has endured on the very site where it was built near the boom-bust mining communities of Westcliffe and Silvercliffe, Colorado. Occupied until 1991 by kin to that first family, it is listed on both the Colorado and National Registers of Historic Places.

History from shore to shore in America is not all that old when we glimpse the big picture, but it is rich and precious to our countrymen. No accounting of our first-tilled fruits would be complete without giving nod to log cabins. As a nation, those dwellings will always romance our collective subconscious.

Pioneer modesty reconnects us to our roots, and while few care to retrieve the fears and hardship of life on hostile frontiers, many yearn for the perceived simplicity of that existence. Most pioneer cabins were necessarily small because logs are heavy and manpower was often limited to the family at hand. Many began as one-room cabins with walls measuring sixteen to eighteen feet across. Those same cabins would often shelter a dozen kids. The family worked, played, ate, and slept together because there was no place else to go. Forced by circumstance to be close, families desperately depended on each other. Today, though we don't honestly need each other like that, in the nostalgic corners of our hearts, we'd like to.

Specialists will advise you that taking on a log restoration presents its own special set of challenges. The process of restoration begs a certain level of integrity. That cabins often will be modified, enlarged, or modernized is understood, but preserving a sense of history and the legacy of lives lived before has special significance. Finishing off a cabin with old materials and old-world craftsmanship may be more than a matter of respect; some see it as duty. Unfortunately, it is also the main reason most restorations cost far more to see through than their contemporary counterparts. Asphalt shingles, cinderblock foundations, and wall-to-wall

carpeting would be poor substitutes for shake roofs, solid-stone chimneys and foundations, and heart-pine floors.

The recipe for restoration begins with the discovery of a sound log structure. Sleuthing ability, personality, and luck may all come into play. Maps of early settlement areas, courthouse records, advertisements, door knocking, schmoozing, and, occasionally, a good jug of hooch might help move you along, but

ABOVE This rustic kitchen nudges up against a tiny two-room cabin in Virginia's Blue Ridge Mountains. Fired up by the triumphant rays of a setting sun, it won't be long before this room's earthly light gives way to the warmth and glow from candles and the potbellied stove.

whatever your approach, Charles McRaven, author of *Building the Hewn Log House,* advises you to have plenty of time and gas.

The most obvious log structures have already been found, so a serious house hunter is likely to putter down countless miles of uncertain road. Keep a sharp eye out for logs in disguise. Siding can hide the object of your quest, but small windows, thick jambs, and stone chimneys are potential clues. Don't assume that logs under wrap are always sound. Many a hopeful enthusiast has bought a house on pure speculation, only to discover that the logs are rotten, termite-chewed, or have been hacked to pieces in the process of a remodel. Poke, prod, and pry your way around a site. If old houses elude you, consider barns, corncribs, and other miscellaneous outbuildings for pleasing time-worn wood.

What you pay for a cabin can vary as much as the people you're

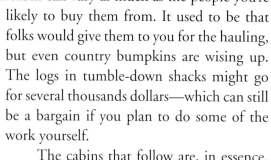

likely to buy them from. It used to be that folks would give them to you for the hauling, but even country bumpkins are wising up. The logs in tumble-down shacks might go for several thousands dollars—which can still be a bargain if you plan to do some of the work yourself.

The cabins that follow are, in essence, the original hands-on log houses. Most have been delivered from uncertain fates by owners and artisans who have given and gained much in the process of imparting new life to old wood (or, in the case of one mountain-man remake, imparting old age to new wood). Skilled craftsmen frequently directed the restoration work, and these cabins were not inexpensive to build. On the contrary, owners driven by a desire to meet the past head-on actually spent more in their pursuit of excellence and authenticity. To meet that challenge was their greater reward.

. . . .

ABOVE Early settlers crammed a variety of earthy fillers between their logs. Sticks, stones, mud, straw, and boards were among the most common. Fieldstones mixed with mortar fill the gaps in this restoration—an uncommon variation sometimes referred to as "pebble chink."

RIGHT Trip Muth was putting the final coat of chink between the 150-year-old oak logs of his Pennsylvania cabin when he discovered a cavity still filled with mud and hay. Prying the debris out with his screwdriver, he found a tiny bundle, neatly wrapped and tied with a bow. It turned out to be the rattle from an eleven-year-old snake. More intriguing than valuable, the hidden memento inspired Trip to carve dates and insert his own provocative time capsules into the building.

People often imagine that disassembling and moving an old log relic might rile up a ghost or two. When the cabin resurrected for William and Marise Craig was nearly complete, neighbors noticed lights coming on at strange hours of the night when the owners were gone. They were concerned enough to call in the electric company, but the phenomenon was never explained. If ghosts were stirring then, they must have been content with the Craigs and their updated haven because they haven't been heard from since.

Having vacationed in Madison County from the time they were newlyweds, the Craigs had talked for more than twenty-five years about owning and eventually retiring to their own place in the Blue Ridge Mountains.

They bought property but weren't sure what they were going to build—until they received a letter from Noah Bradley of Blue Mountain Builders. On one of Noah's regular forays to the county courthouse, he discovered that the Craigs owned land, and he approached them with a convincing case for old logs.

The family agreed on a traditional one-over-one design where Marise says they could spend their time enjoying the outdoors instead of cleaning. Historically, a tiny cabin like this would harbor the story of long-suffering pioneers and a dozen or so children raised inside. One room upstairs was for sleeping, while the single room downstairs was for everything else. If a family was able, they might eventually add a board lean-to on back for the kitchen. A separate cooking area would keep the rest of the house from overheating in summer. The Craigs' lean-to is of new logs but was so skillfully blended into the old that you wouldn't notice.

During the course of construction, Bill took time off from his job at the Pentagon to mix mortar and schlep rock with the crew. This cabin would be a place where memories were made, and pride of ownership would

William and Marise Craig
DHUINCRAG
LOCATION: Madison, Virginia
SIZE: 829 sq. ft.
COST: $110,000 ($130/sq. ft.)
BUILDING TIME: 1995 (8 months)
ADVICE: It's hard to get a contract
price on a restoration, so trust your
instincts and work with people
in whom you believe.

come through family involvement in the building process. After the logs were up, the Craigs and their two teenage children pitched in as often as they could on weekends. They cleaned the site, stripped and refinished old doors and floors, and painted trim. There was a learning curve involved, and Marise recalls how she inadvertently painted all the windows shut. Sometime later, Bill and a member of Noah's crew put up a second 10-by-16-foot 1700s-vintage log cabin. Bill and Marise finished off the erected shell by themselves and now keep yard tools and miscellaneous overflow inside.

Taking on their cabin project without the expertise and craftsmanship of Noah's experienced crew would have been unthinkable for the Craigs. However, that put them in a situation where the cost per square foot was substantial. While Noah always tours his clients through past projects and reveals their costs, he says it is very difficult to bid a new project with complete accuracy. It's a "create-as-you-go" building process, and antique materials must be secured along the way. Sometimes there is no way of knowing where you'll find them, what condition they will be in, or how much you'll have to pay. He says, "I've found rock for free, and I've paid $375 per ton for it." Transporting materials from remote locations, then cleaning, pulling old nails, trimming waste, and refitting old wood is a reliably unpredictable chore. That was the case here, and the contracted price didn't hold. Noah responded by working on a "time and materials basis." Billings were sent every two weeks along with copies of receipts for materials and subcontractors and a breakdown of his crew's hours and payment schedules.

FAR LEFT William and Marise Craig both hail from Scottish ancestry so they chose to name their cozy retreat "Dhuincrag." The term is a Gaelic one meaning "fortress on a rocky hill." Not only is it aptly named because the gentle hills fall away below them, but in June of 1995, just two days after they moved in, much of the valley floor was ravaged by a millennium flood. Some of their friends and closest neighbors lost nearly everything, but their hilltop cabin, fortified against the storm, was safe and dry.

LEFT "Naily pine" is the local name given to wood branded by the dark trailings of old nails removed in the process of re-milling. That characteristic wood lines this bathroom wall. The leaded-glass window was once at home in an English church.

BELOW A spacious bedroom takes up the second story and is filled with family heirlooms that relate to the hat- and shoe-making trades of certain ancestors. The bed, once belonging to Marise's grandparents, is covered with a Jacquard coverlet that has been in her family since the 1860s. The immigrant trunk is their linen closet, and Marise's great-grandmother's shoes are displayed on top.

RIGHT Black-and-white pictures of Marise's ancestors fill scrapbooks and dress the walls of their history-laden cabin. Some of them date to the 1800s and show proud kinfolk who raised their own families in the shelter of logs. The Craigs' own wooden walls are oak and chestnut. Sound and seasoned for more than a century, nails will scarcely penetrate them.

Even today, some lending institutions may find all this a little unsettling. The Craigs' mainstream, multistate bank was unfamiliar with log restorations and would not agree to a construction loan. The family replied by approaching a local bank in the neighborhood of the cabin. They met with success but point out that owning their land outright helped.

This cabin is their own little piece of heaven, and while they have yet to retire, Marise believes she could spend the rest of her life here. "We come every single weekend," she says, adding, "I'm afraid that we'll be getting ready to leave for home one Sunday, and I'm just not going to go!"

ABOVE After the mountain-top cabin burned in 1988 (see black-and-white photo to the right), this second poplar-and-chestnut cabin was adopted by the family. In the process of restoring it, the crew discovered that the logs were spiked in the corners with "common" nails not largely available until the turn of the twentieth century. Knowing that the logs were far older, they surmised the cabin had been moved. Later, they discovered that a "mean gully washer" had forced earlier occupants to relocate on higher ground.

(ORIGINAL CABIN DESTROYED BY FIRE)

VIRGINIA FAMILY CABIN
LOCATION: Madison County, Virginia
SIZE: 1,680 sq. ft. plus partial basement
COST: $300,000 for two-story mountaintop cabin ($142/sq. ft.)
BUILDING TIME: 1994
ADVICE: Persist! Old trees bear precious new fruit.

Old homes are about history—the history of families. Floors worn thin by the knees of fire tenders and women cooking at the hearth; the etchings of mischievous children in walls built of logs; the vanishing remnants of grave markers out back—we look for those things and want so badly to glimpse the lives of able-bodied people who lived before us in a land so familiar yet utterly changed. We don't often think about our own daily lives as having historical merit, but someday they will. As we pick up the pieces of a forgotten homestead, change the scenery, and recast the characters, we may perpetuate the history of others, but we are also making our own. While no one can say how the story goes two hundred years from now, we visited one extended Washington, D.C., family that has been adding to memories of old and fashioning new ones on a Madison County mountaintop since the mid-1950s.

This particular story began with the purchase of an abandoned chestnut cabin that had already cradled at least nine babies, certainly by then all great-grandparents, if they were still alive. The little cottage was had for $75, and a logger was hired to winch disassembled and numbered logs from the bottom of the mountain to the top. Building with logs was nearly a lost art in the fifties, but after some searching, the family routed out an "old codger" who could still recall the workings of broadaxes, drawknives, and chisels. About $1,500 later, the rustic cabin was reborn into the lives of this new

family who would vacation there faithfully for more than thirty-five years. The couple's own five children would grow up on the crown of that hill, claiming the woods, fields, springs, and boundless views as their very own. A family journal was kept and the years recorded week by week, month by month, year by year.

Then on July 11, 1988, lightning struck, and the cabin burned to the ground. The news was received in a flood of tears. Gone was the wellspring of family unity—the place where parents, children, and grandchildren were drawn together through time and circumstance. It had been their "emotional core."

Some years passed as the family regrouped, but they never stopped coming up the mountain. For a while they brought tents and camped out. Then, not far away and lost to the labors of neglect, a new cabin was discovered. Overgrown with honeysuckle, the roof had caved in, the porch had sagged, and the chimney had crumbled. Determined to bring the family back together round a common hearth, they called in seven different contractors to restore their find. Each contractor claimed the job impossible. Knock it down, push it over, and never mind, they said. But the family would not, and on their eighth go-around, they found Noah Bradley and his company, Blue Mountain Builders.

LEFT So often our forebears didn't lay foundations under their homes. That's why so many homes gave way to rot and termites. Sitting atop teetery columns of dry-stacked rocks, this cabin has one-upped less-successful relations. Noah restored it the way it stood. The ash floor of the cabin was left in place, then reinforced and insulated from beneath.

The cabin was part chestnut and part poplar. Not everyone likes poplar, says Noah, but the old-growth wood is light, the logs large, and time erodes them smooth and soft like rocks. It's marvelous! He accepted the challenge and in the end hadn't replaced a single log.

For the family, that cabin and Blue Mountain Builders signaled a new beginning. Firelight danced once again on handworked wood. Guitars, laughter, and song mingled with the scent of wild blueberry pancakes. Not only had the family repaired the hole in their collective heart, but they now knew a builder who could be trusted to re-create a cabin like the one they had lost to fire.

Noah did just that, working with oak logs from an 18-by-24-foot, two-and-a-half-story home dating from the mid-1800s. At first the cabin was to be very rustic, much like the retreat it was replacing. But the family had aged and grown. There were grandparents, spouses, and babies. Finally, designed by committee, the cabin that emerged had a partial basement, two plumbed baths, a finished attic complete with dormers, a modern kitchen, laundry facilities, and wraparound porches. It was generations removed from its predecessor, but in the continuum of time it was just right.

Delighted by the craftsmanship of Noah's dedicated crew, the family's rever-

ence for forgotten structures deepened. A barn was resurrected, and then a five-story, eleven-sided silo. Oh, the silo, chuckles the family patriarch—that was pure folly! It had been discovered on the brink of destruction. Built entirely of extinct chestnut, the family couldn't bear to see the fire department burn it down for practice. They bought it and sent Blue Mountain Builders to the rescue. The crew disassembled the tower board by board—more than 2,000 of them! Ten thousand nails were removed and a limestone foundation meticulously shaped and stacked to accommodate the oddly configured granary in its new location.

Finished with fifteen red-trimmed windows and a glass-enclosed observation deck forty-eight feet above the ground, the silo is a place to be and to remember. A ladder built into one wall climbs straight to the top, bypassing five floors. Look down if you dare. While the older generation delights in the view and perhaps the chance to meditate, the younger one thrills at the challenge of racing up and down the ticklish ladder, playing hide-and-seek, or inventing games about imaginary impenetrable fortresses, prisoners in distress, and daring rescues. The family, the fire, the cabins, the silo: they are all part of a story that will travel down the mountain and across the barriers of time into history.

BOTTOM LEFT The setting sun engulfs the new mountaintop cabin in dazzling bursts of light. Sleeping porches face a view that spans three counties. In summer storms, the heaven-high hill sparks with electricity, but the cabin—built of solid wood and natural stone, and having a copper roof with several well-placed lightning rods—should safely endure for another 300 years.

TOP LEFT A single bedroom takes up most of the second floor in the new cabin. A stone fireplace is flued into the massive chimney that rises so prominently along the outside wall. The mantel was carved with a honeysuckle motif by a crewman, who also fashioned the door, its latch, and the wooden hinges from salvaged heart pine.

BELOW Blue Mountain Builders has dubbed this eleven-sided silo an "undecagon." Why eleven sides when eight or twelve would have been the norm? No one is quite sure, but Noah surmises that a farmer, working during the Great Depression in the 1930s, laid out a circle on the ground 12 feet in diameter (a common dimension for silos). Then he cut standard 8- or 16-foot lengths of chestnut lumber into 4-foot boards. He came up with eleven sides without wasting a lick of wood.

FAR RIGHT Black Cat Cabin's namesake is the road that runs through this once-rural neighborhood of small family-owned farms. Some of those families are black descendants of freed slaves whose bittersweet history lingers in the stirrings of ancient oaks. All is changing now. Many of the farms are gone and a housing development is slated 360 degrees around Julie's cabin. There is pressure to sell, and one day the cabin may be replaced with something more elegant but probably soulless.

BELOW When black men and white turned out for a hard-drinking, high-rolling night at the lodge, trouble usually wasn't far behind. In those days, the front door, still fixed with its original deadbolt hardware, was barricaded shut with a hefty board jammed across cast-iron brackets. A ceramic viper appraises friend or foe from the Adirondack-style catchall at the entrance.

Julie Stein
BLACK CAT CABIN
LOCATION: Keswick, Virginia
SIZE: 2,192 sq. ft.
COST: $80,000 for addition and restoration ($36/sq. ft.)
BUILDING TIME: 1990
ADVICE: Have an old house inspected before you buy.

Memories of a murky past may linger in the shadows of Black Cat Cabin, but its enigmatic history adds color and intrigue. Built in the 1930s, about the same time as the exclusive Keswick Country Club nearby, the cabin hosted hunters and poker players—be they white men or black. Free-flowing whiskey, loose women, and integrated play behind closed doors set the stage for violent altercations—not so much among patrons as between them and disapproving core-Southern thinkers.

Today, vague tales of suicide and uncertain death are enthusiastically recounted by little old gray-haired neighbors. While owner Julie Stein is amused by the mystery of the place, she was taken in by something entirely different.

She was in her early twenties when she first saw the cabin under a silent blanket of critter-tracked snow. Deer, wild turkeys, foxes, owls, and hawks laid claim to the eight-and-a-half acres of surrounding woods. The miniature lodge, long neglected by humans, was redone to the likes of less tidy families of bats, squirrels, woodpeckers, and copperhead snakes. To Julie it was neither creepy nor dreary. Mesmerized by the solitude, it was love at first site, and she bought the place before fully realizing how much it would cost to reconcile it as her home.

On closer inspection, she discovered that the logs were laying on bare ground. Cement slathered around the base of the building hid foundation logs that were so punky you could push your finger right in. There was no insulation in the ceiling, and inside, the tin roof was plainly visible through widely spaced rafters. The kitchen needed to be gutted and redone along with all the wiring and plumbing. Floors, vents, air conditioning, and a dozen other matters needed attention before the remake was complete.

Julie hired local craftsman Charles McRaven to handle the restoration work and build a 290-square-foot hand-hewn addition on the end of the house. Work began by jacking up the entire building one section at a time, replacing rotten logs (in some cases several courses deep), and constructing a new stone foundation. As work progressed, even McRaven, a veteran artisan and published author on hewn

RIGHT When Julie bought the cabin, the right-hand window on the bathroom wall glimpsed wooded acreage outside. Now the new addition stands next door, and the window has been cleverly converted to a medicine chest. Pale yellow paint brightens the log walls and tub, and afternoon sun shimmers in the folds of a burnt velvet curtain draped loosely over a dogwood branch.

BELOW In the master bedroom upstairs, a path of windows traces the outline of the gable end. On steamy summer nights, Julie props them open with dowels and is lulled off to sleep by the songs of tree frogs performing in her woods. Much of her free time is spent with the horses she keeps on her property, and a usin' collection of western cowboy boots reflects her fascination with both the animals and western lore.

homes and stone masonry, had not fully anticipated the depth of decay. Apart from logs decomposing on the ground, termites had eaten their way around door and window frames, then moved into adjacent walls. In reality, the cabin was one good wind away from firewood, and McRaven says it was one of the most challenging restoration projects he has undertaken. As so often happens with this kind of work, labor costs went out the window, and the final bill was nearly double that of earlier projections.

Working with pine logs dismantled from another 150-year-old cabin, the hewn addition went up more predictably. The new section included 216 square feet in a single room downstairs, plus a narrow bath upstairs adjacent to the master bedroom. Chinking was knocked out of the existing cabin and the new logs notched into the old. McRaven says the key was using logs of similar size. Inside, overhead beams came from yet another house. Had the addition been any larger they would have been too small. In Virginia and certainly in other areas of the

country, building codes demand that old wood be certified by an engineer for structural integrity. Recycled ceiling beams and floor joists might not meet current standards for weight-bearing loads. Likewise, McRaven says, antiquated stairways may be too steep and narrow or doorways too low.

Julie Stein's building retains its original tin roof, but spaces between log rafters were filled with foam insulation and covered with Sheetrock. The tin got a new coat of color, and the trim on reframed door and window openings was painted to match. An existing oil furnace is still used occasionally for backup heat, but Julie had wood-burning stoves inserted into the cabin's two massive rock fireplaces. Now she heats almost exclusively with wood.

Julie has her master's degree in conservation biology, so it's not surprising that she has a tender place in her heart for the creatures that once made her house their own. When she finally moved in, a small

colony of bats still slept behind kitchen cupboards that had yet to be replaced. At night, with many of their old escape routes blocked off, some would become trapped in her bedroom upstairs. The unlikely housemates were always rescued, and for a while Julie slept with the doors and windows propped open on their behalf.

Outside, the tangled woodscape concealed more surprises. All over the property, says Julie, were found horseshoes bedded in cement and poised for good luck. Maybe, she laughs, they were there to ward away evil spirits, but she's not sure they worked. In fact, after all of Julie's efforts, Black Cat Cabin faces an uncertain future. The floundering Keswick Country Club has since been restored even beyond its former elegance and an exclusive golf course has been developed. Blue-blooded development is closing in around the cabin, and the whole area will soon be part of a secured community. Already, she says, her woods are less wild, and while her property may be more valuable now, that isn't what brought her, nor is it what will keep her here.

ABOVE Western artifacts, Adirondack camp pieces, and the trappings of Appalachia fill the rooms in Julie's cabin to overflowing. Rich fabrics and vivid works of collectible art brighten typically dark interiors. Many of her furnishings and accessories came from junking expeditions in the Blue Ridge Mountains.

RIGHT A century-old split-rail chestnut fence borders the Altaffers' even-older log cabin. Christened "Doubleview" for its vista of Double Top and Old Rag Mountains across the valley, Larry thinks of ships and oceans when he watches fog roll in from its massive two-story front porch.

**Dr. and Mrs.
Lawrence F. Altaffer III
DOUBLEVIEW**
LOCATION: Madison County,
Virginia
SIZE: 1,664 sq. ft. plus attic loft
COST: $300,000 ($150/sq. ft.)
BUILDING TIME: 1989–1990
(14 months)
ADVICE: Take delight in the
details, and honor history with
an eye toward accuracy.

America was launched from eastern shores, and there are families who dug their heels in and never left. Often one generation followed the next, adding its own distinct but traceable link in the family chain. Lawrence Altaffer III and his wife come from stout lines of historic eastern stock. Mrs. Altaffer's kin are heirs to Mount Airy, a famous old Virginia plantation that has been passed down from father to son since 1660. Larry, likewise, has tracked his roots from the village of William Tell in Switzerland to American soil in 1730, where his ancestors migrated to Virginia's Shenandoah Valley and laid anchor. Born and bred to cherish the tracings of time, the Altaffers took special pleasure in finding and restoring a little chunk of eighteenth-century American lore.

Their two-and-a-half-story hewn-log house dates back to the 1700s. Measuring 32-by-26 feet, it is larger than the cabins typically built by pioneer families with their limited resources and manpower. It is believed instead to have been a garrison house in a Virginia fort burned by Indians in 1790. Having survived the holocaust, it was later disassembled and moved about a mile downhill to territory that would be claimed by West Virginia during the Civil War. Plastered inside and covered over with weatherboarding, logs vanished beneath the gentility of a fine family home for nearly 150 years. Ultimately, time took its toll, and the house was given over to hay storage. Its original double chimneys were dismantled and the stones carted off. The cabin was spared

the pyre a second time when Tom Thorpe, a veteran house hunter, rescued it from a farmer who wanted a new barn made from metal.

Always intending to have their own hewn-log retreat one day, the Altaffers purchased land on a wooded mountaintop in the Virginia Blue Ridge. Larry had been on a house-hunting pilgrimage for nearly two years when he heard about Tom's find. Built entirely from oak, bits and pieces of the cabin's history were revealed in its construction. Hand-forged nails told of an eighteenth-century birthing, while further clues, including charred logs and cut nails

BELOW Dr. Altaffer was delighted to be able to fill his period cabin with some of the authentic trappings of eighteenth- and nineteenth-century living. Included in the historic harvest of collections from the Shenandoah Valley and southern Pennslyvania are primitive folk art, miniature log cabins, hand-carved bears, primitive instruments, and stoneware fashioned by Larry's own acclaimed Great-great-great-uncle Emanuel Suter.

RIGHT Tin and metal sprout up around the Altaffers' historic cabin before renovation in a setting that has grown impatient with its architectural forebear. Rescue came just in the nick of time.

BELOW A newfangled meter box is an ugly thing on an old log cabin. Larry wanted to put his inside, but the electric company wouldn't hear of it. Instead, Blue Mountain Builders fashioned a rustic cabinet to hide it.

dating from the Civil War, suggested its move, second raising, and probable expansion. The Altaffers hired Noah Bradley and the crew of Blue Mountain Builders to put it up for the third time. Given the toil of building these homes more than a century ago, it was often easier to dismantle one and move it than to start from scratch. They were the original mobile homes, says Noah, who has seen dozens of examples in his backwoods search for the objects of his trade.

All the pieces of the cabin were carefully marked before it was taken apart and moved to the Altaffer's site. Craftsmen pieced it back together as coded, with one notable exception: the second floor was spun 180 degrees so that the existing door would face the picture-perfect view of Double Top Mountain leafing into sky and mist above orchards, quaint cottages, and lightly trod country roads. The house was perched on an arched rock foundation and its double chimneys restored. Nearly 400 tons of fossil-imprinted West Virginia sandstone was salvaged from other fallen chimneys to complete that work.

The Altaffers lived about an hour and a half away in Fredericksburg. Larry came up every Tuesday through fourteen months of construction to watch the progress and work through new ideas with

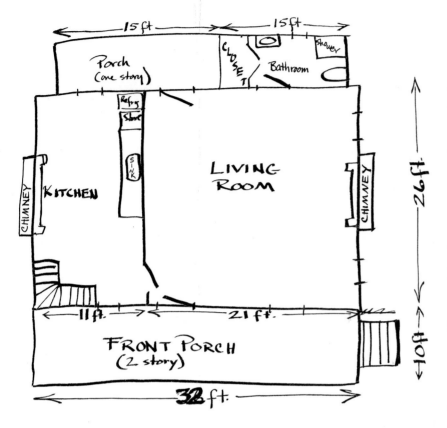

DOUBLEVIEW — FIRST FLOOR

15 ft — 15 ft

Porch (one story)

CLOSET

Bathroom

Shower

Refrig

Stove

SINK

KITCHEN

CHIMNEY

LIVING ROOM

CHIMNEY

26 ft

10 ft

11 ft — 21 ft

FRONT PORCH (2 story)

32 ft

the crew. "Noah's men," says Larry, "took tremendous pride in their work. I had never built a house before, and sometimes they would diplomatically pick at me to let them do it right." Larry was so engaged by the whole process that he says he suffered post-construction blues when the cabin was finished.

He didn't stay down for long. Believing that if you really want to touch the past you have to experience it, he adventures out to eighteenth-century camping reenactments at mountain-man rendezvous with his family. He has also collected the accouterments of early hearth cooking and mastered the skills. Now he passes fun and knowledge along to groups of Scouts and school children who come to visit. Hovering around an old-fashioned tin reflector oven and hanging plate warmers in his walk-in kitchen fireplace, Larry will demonstrate how to spit roast a squirrel, then serve it up with all the fixin's and a bellyful of history!

RIGHT The Altaffer family has forged its own bit of history on the wall. Handprints and a date commemorating the home's completion will read like pages from a book to future historians. Characteristically wide chink lines are filled with beige-colored mortar. While newer synthetic chinking products are more popular, Blue Mountain Builders would walk away from a job before using something so "plastic" on a restoration.

Stuart and Mary Thompson Family
LOCATION: Pinedale, Wyoming
SIZE: 2,400 sq. ft.
COST: $92/sq. ft.
BUILDING TIME: 1990–1991
ADVICE: Poor design or lack of
planning will be your Achilles' heel.
Consider site, function,
and resources first.

ABOVE Summer days are cherished in Wyoming, where the locals profess there are only two seasons: winter and July/August. When the sun shines, the Thompson children make their own hay selling lemonade.

In 1975 Stuart and Mary Thompson were living the enviable life of western youth. Winters found them working and skiing in a popular resort town, while in warm weather they traded ski boots for cowboy boots and wrangled their way across the wide-open, cattle-grazed Wyoming plains. By then Stuart had also done some log-home construction, and it was during that year that he and Mary decided to go official and call themselves Logcrafters. Today they are still in busi-

ness and have perfected what they call a super-insulated "sandwich wall" log home. Generally they use this system to build new homes, but when they bought a dilapidated 1920s log house for themselves, they employed it in the restoration.

Sandwich construction begins with an outer wall built with logs sawn on three sides in the shape of a D. Next comes foam insulation with an air-infiltration barrier, then a stud wall insulated with fiberglass. A vapor barrier goes over that, and an interior veneer of thinner-cut logs finishes it off. The result is an airtight, super-energy-efficient system that resembles a solid log wall but is actually a log wall and a conventionally framed wall sandwiched together. Though more expensive to build, this double-wall system saves many heating and cooling dollars each year.

Because Wyoming pioneers had access to sawmills, they were building with D logs early in the twentieth century. Many of the buildings in the nearby town of Pinedale were built that way, then covered over—including the home that Mary and Stuart stumbled across while hunting for property. "It was wrapped in mint green siding," says Mary, "but it had a beautiful form." Having been abused by negligent renters for many years, it was in terrible shape. Restoring it turned out to be a monumental chore, and Stuart says they could have built the same thing for less if they had just invited the volunteer fire department over for a marshmallow roast. Mary chuckles but insists that the

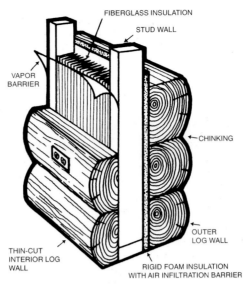

FIBERGLASS INSULATION

STUD WALL

VAPOR BARRIER

CHINKING

THIN-CUT INTERIOR LOG WALL

OUTER LOG WALL

RIGID FOAM INSULATION WITH AIR INFILTRATION BARRIER

Illustration courtesy Logcrafters

BELOW The front porch on the original house wasn't covered, nor was there a dormer above it. Both features were built for function but give this farmhouse added charm.

house has historical merit, and she felt an obligation to preserve what bit of it they could. Besides, they had no home at the time and believed they could live there during renovation.

That turned out to be their first overly optimistic assumption. When they started tearing fiberboard down to get at the guts of the house, the electrical system they exposed was scary. Bare copper wire was stapled to rafters charred black in half a dozen places. Not willing to chance it all to fire, they spent the year on-site in a sheep wagon. When it came right down to it, there wasn't much of the house they could save outside of the log walls, and before they were through, more than a hundred pickup loads of irreparable history had gone to the dump.

The logs, however, were in good shape with the exception of poorly done butt-and-pass corners. Some of them had not been peeled, and though they weren't rotten, the Thompsons sawed them flush with the house and capped them with corner boards. Iron must have been at a premium when the house was built, because the logs were not spiked and there were only a handful of nails used in constructing the roof. To hold the logs in place during the restoration, the Thompsons screwed on sheets of plywood. They covered that with house wrap, then built up the walls using the principles of sandwich construction. On the inside, they

LEFT You can warm your backside at a seat-high hearth shared by both the kitchen and living room. Cedar beams overhead are antiqued and hand-brushed with a light wash. The kitchen cabinets, also built from cedar, are worked over with a four-step process using layers of blue and white paint. Mary, who is skilled at creating antique game boards like those in the kitchen, did most of this work.

RIGHT The second story in the original farmhouse was not built from logs, and on closer inspection, there was little of it worth saving. When it was reframed, two new dormers were added: one to accommodate new back-to-back bathrooms, and another in this master bedroom to let in sunlight, create headroom, and give an architectural face-lift to the front of the house.

finished some of the walls with a thin veneer of logs and completed others with stucco and paint.

The house is heated by a central, thermostatically controlled, wood-burning fireplace. River-rock hearths face the kitchen on one side and the living room on the other. Regulated amounts of outside air are pulled into the sealed combustion firebox. A separate system circulates air around the firebox, then forces it out into the living space. Because sandwich-wall design permits the construction of a virtually airtight home, stale air must be refreshed regularly. In this house, that is accomplished through a heat recovery and ventilation system that transfers warmth from the stale air it exhausts to the fresh air it brings back in. An add-on sunroom is also part of this multifarious system. The house is many times more efficient than a comparable, traditional log home. At an elevation of 8,000 feet in an area averaging only thirty frost-free days a year, this family gets by with less than one cord of wood annually.

In the original design, living space considered ample by 1920s standards was cramped and awkward. Without altering the original footprint, the Thompsons opened and updated claustrophobic areas upstairs and under the house. The basic footprint included about 825 square feet on the main floor plus an atticlike second story. The house sat atop a semifinished, forehead-high cellar. Though grungy and littered with the desiccated carcasses of frogs and mice, the Thompsons saw a usable basement in their future. They jacked up the entire house and added eighteen more inches to the existing foundation. By raising the ceilings, Mary and Stuart converted the 775-square-foot cellar into a family room, guest bedroom, laundry facility, and pantry.

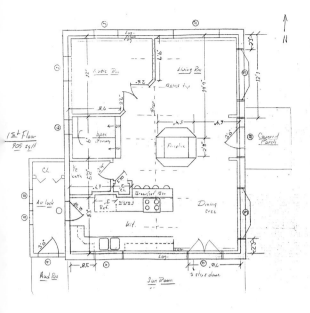

Six hundred and forty acres surround this resurrected farmhouse where the Thompsons raise cattle, board horses, and operate their company. As the season changes, Wyoming winds blow away summer and churn the plains like butter. But buttoned up, this red-roofed cottage will ease this family and those who follow through countless winters to come.

BELOW Bays were not original to this 1920s home, but window openings on either side of the front door were the right size to accommodate them. Nearly all the low-E windows came from a manufacturer who practically gave them away when Stuart explained that they would be using this home as their company's showpiece. They ended up with $35,000 worth of "seconds" for $5,000. Bay windows were not included, so Stuart had to puzzle them together from miscellaneous sections.

RIGHT At a glance, this crouching cabin might appear to harbor a strong-smelling hermit. Closer inspection reveals otherwise. For starters, it actually has a double roof with two sets of purlins. This was done to make the roof profile appear thin from the outside, while allowing space inside for insulation and fire sprinklers. The ceiling is dropped down fifteen inches and supported by a second set of purlins that doesn't extend through the walls.

Photograph © Dave Marlow

Photograph courtesy Eagle County Historical Society

(CABIN BASED ON THIS PHOTO & OTHERS)
BABY BEAR CABIN
LOCATION: Near Aspen, Colorado
SIZE: 500 sq. ft.
COST: $500/sq. ft.
BUILDING TIME: 1993–1996
ADVICE: Imagination and craftsmanship go hand in hand. Don't underestimate the power or importance of either.

This "mountain man" cabin is not old, but the owners took great care to make it look and feel that way. Like a good book, you can lose yourself in the adventure of it all. And, like a tale in the making, this cabin was authored, chapter by chapter, through the careful research and playful deliberation of its owners.

In the beginning there was just a longing. As avid hikers and backpackers, the owners frequently stumbled across the forgotten shelters of miners, trappers, and (don't you suppose) outlaws, too. What would it be like to walk through such a door and call it home? A vision took root, and the family spent six years looking for land with a cabin on it that could be restored. When nothing turned up, they realized they would have to create their own.

The couple bought land in the mountains above Aspen, Colorado, then set about the edifying task of searching out the hows, whats, and whys of a genuine 1890s prospector's cabin. The historical society was a wellspring of information. Black-and-white photos of craggy-faced, gun-toting men poised by their squat-bodied shelters served as the family's first blueprints.

As a business consultant for a pharmaceutical company, the husband was content to direct the creative process and hire others who could build his imagined hideaway. Unlike those boom-bust cabins of old, this refuge would not be a hurried affair. Though outwardly genuine, this 500-square-foot history book remake would have to conceal all the conveniences of the modern world within its rough-cut walls and boot-worn floors. In the end, it would include amenities like radiant-heat floors, a wine cellar, and an automated sprinkler system hidden in the roof. The cabin was "outrageously expensive" to build, confides the owner, but he was prepared for that. This wasn't about money, rather "it was a voyage of discovery."

The search for a builder eventually ended at the doorstep of a Colorado handcrafter named Ed Shure. An architect was also called upon to lay out working drawings—not an easy task in Aspen, laughs the owner, where anything under 8,000 square feet turns up disinterested yawns. One, Michael Gassman, didn't yawn. Instead, the two of them revisited shelters of the Old West. They studied movies like *Jeremiah Johnson,* then debated such cabiny traits as window size, roof angle, and room proportion.

The owner orchestrated the whole event and combed the country, casting for the right building materials, fixtures,

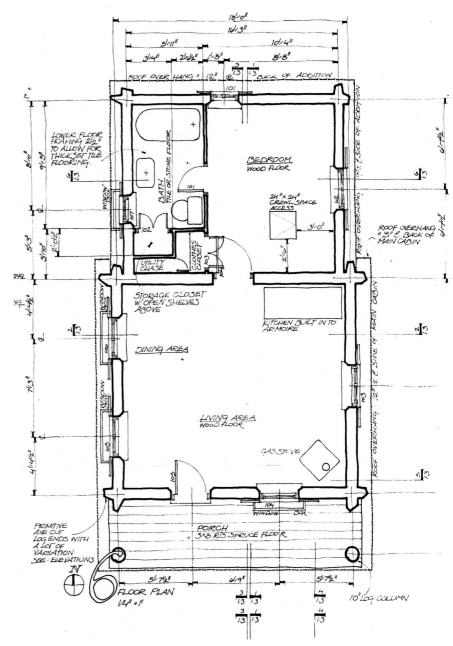

and furniture. He found an elderly woodsman, who had once done reproduction work for museums, to split huge thirty-two-inch shakes for the roof. Another problem was solved in Oregon, where the owner turned up a potion to chemically age knots and fresh-cut log ends. Stain, already tried, had been dismissed as "hokey."

The windows came from Georgia and the floors from an ailing Virginia

RIGHT The family wanted an indoor bathroom but was faced with the dilemma of what kind to put in a cabin that wouldn't have had one. "In the end, we 'borrowed' a Victorian look," says the owner. It's not the same place, but it is the same time period.

BELOW The doorway to Baby Bear Cabin frames Hayden Peak in the distance, and local wildlife still claim this territory for themselves. Shoes left on the porch are likely to become chew toys for the resident fox, while the neighborhood black bear seems to think he should be on the guest list for dinner.

farmhouse. A craftsman in Connecticut built a freestanding armoire to hide the entire kitchen! Since you wouldn't find a dishwasher or microwave oven in an 1890s cabin, these are incognito, as are the stovetop, sink, toaster oven, and a mini fridge (complete with ice maker) imported from England. The fridge uses something called "absorption technology." There is no motor or compressor, so it doesn't make a sound. All that, and a pantry too, is bundled up in a dinged and hand-rubbed cabinet in the living part of the two-room cabin.

There are other surprises as well. A trapdoor under a rug in the bedroom leads down awkward steps to a hair-height cellar. There reside a washer/dryer, full-size refrigerator, the mechanical workings of the radiant-heat floors, and an ample

wine cellar. The electrical box is down there, too, and getting that approved was more luck than not (stairs too steep, ceiling too low, etc.). As it turns out, the building inspector recalled a nearby cabin he had personally wired more than thirty years ago. That cabin has since disappeared into the belly of a new 12,000-square-foot log house, but the memory of the place was enough to guide the inspector to a forgiving paragraph in his code book having something to do with "alternative methods."

The cottage itself is built with dead-standing, Swedish-coped logs. Because those first cabins were usually plugged with mud and grass, not mortar, the owners didn't want visible chink lines. Far more sophisticated than anything a trapper might put up in haste, the notch work and joinery was a process the husband relished. "I'm a very hands-on type of guy," he says, and explains that while he's always enjoyed his business, he never stopped to wonder

why. After working on the cabin, he realized his enjoyment all boiled down to learning new things, concocting novel solutions, and experiencing the camaraderie of laboring alongside people who really excel at their work. And while this little retreat is steeped in a world of make-believe, the owner confesses that in many ways it has been a metaphor for his life. With genuine delight, he proclaims, "This is where I found out about myself!"

ABOVE On a reconnaissance trip to search out old wood, the owner found a miller who was converting hand-hewn oak beams into flooring. The hacked outer skins had been discarded as too rough to walk on, but they were perfect for the ceiling! Extra thought went into every detail of the cabin, and, while everything literally is too good to be true, the romance and adventure of the place are deeply satisfying.

David Smith and son
LOCATION: Jackson, Wyoming
SIZE: 1,500 sq. ft., including
loft and basement
BUILDING TIME: 1988
ADVICE: Less is more.

BELOW Although this front porch is an add-on to the original cabin, it is built with old timbers from a wall of the existing home.

A fast-paced life has always been David Smith's beck and call. Fresh out of college, he moved to Africa and worked his way across the continent at a variety of jobs that included commercial bush pilot and freelance photojournalist. He stayed there for eight years, visiting forty-two countries and reporting on three separate skirmishes. His articles and photographs appeared in a number of prominent publications, including the *Washington Post, Newsweek,* and *Paris-Match.* Upon returning to the United States, David took up work in Los Angeles writing screenplays for several major motion-picture studios—in his words,

"less dangerous work, though no less bloody." Today, while still involved with various film projects, David spends more time working on regional conservation issues.

Being a private person, David is reluctant to discuss his "personal ancient history." He'll talk fast with no pause for questions until he gets to the part about Christmas Eve 1988. That was the day he and his young son, Zebediah, moved into his newly restored 18-by-36-foot log cabin. There was plastic insulation covering the entire ceiling and brown paper taped to the unfinished floors. It was Zeb's seventh birthday, and it was snowing.

For David, the memory of that day is still vivid, and in the years since, the place has come to elicit intense personal emotions. The cabin came from Montana. Roofless, it was just taking up space on some rancher's land. Architect Jonathan Foote discovered it, and David contracted with Foote's construction company, On Site Management, to restore it. Of course, the cabin was adapted in the process, but a sense of history and wonder remain. The stories are there—still preserved in the scrapes and hollows of the logs. "Now," says David, "I share a part of that too."

David is the first to tell you that he isn't a builder, but he was on the job nearly

ABOVE Working on-site with the crew was an incredibly meaningful experience, says David. He could be very specific about details and contribute to the design in significant ways. He points to the addition of French doors and the cutaway balcony upstairs as one example.

ABOVE Great care was taken to give this fireplace the simplistic look of dry-stacked rock. In reality, such deception is difficult to pull off. To meet local building and earthquake codes, there is an elaborate concrete-and-steel assembly hidden within.

every day of construction. He remembers working through the fall under blue skies and a canopy of blazing yellow aspens. "I was the go-fer. I got to hump a few logs, pick up stones, and bring pizza and beer to the crew." Even though David respected the talented craftsmen, his being there made all the difference. Every detail was important. He could hand-pick the lintel stone for the fireplace and the log for the mantel. He could brainstorm ideas and tweak the design to get it just right. At one point, he says, "I knew I wanted 6,000,000-year-old Wyoming fish swimming around my bathroom sink." Taking David's idea into the workshop, a local

artisan transformed fossil-rich slabs of Wyoming sandstone into a countertop.

The interior space is small, but there is room enough for everything David needs. And, says David, that comfortable smallness led to one of the most satisfying gatherings he has ever hosted at his home. Through acquaintance and happenstance, David got a phone call one afternoon from the daughter of the former governor of Wyoming. "I hope you don't mind," she said, "but my dad has just invited President Bill Clinton and sixteen of his closest friends and advisors over for dinner at your house!"

Dutifully, the secret service showed

up first. After glancing quickly around, with polite compliments on the property and little cabin, the agents asked David, "Where's the house?" Three hours later, the president and his party arrived for "one" scheduled hour of relaxation. As the sun set, they all hit golf balls off David's bluff. Dinner was served in the backyard, and the group gnawed shamelessly on piles of messy ribs and corn. More than five hours later, they were still there, lounging around a roaring campfire under a starlit sky. When the party finally rose to leave, it was well past midnight.

In parting, the president thanked David for what he called the most relaxing evening he had enjoyed in many months.

David is amused by the recognition that his cabin is probably the smallest residence in modern history to host dinner for a sitting president of the United States. And while something big and shiny might be more impressive, it most likely would not offer up those simpler, soul-settling gifts that make this cabin the special place it is.

BELOW As a dedicated conservationist actively involved in several organizations working to preserve the West's wildlife and diminishing spaces, David is pleased to have been able to "recycle" his unobtrusive cabin on a magnificent bluff overlooking the Snake River. Waking to that morning view, says David, is a near-religious experience.

RIGHT David's affection for African art and culture is evident throughout his cabin. In the loft, those eclectic furnishings combine with oversized windows and beaded-wood doors to create a casual, warm, and rustic atmosphere.

5 IT'S IN THE DETAILS

Most all homebuilders, no matter how modest their cabin in the woods, have champagne taste somewhere along the way. Though you may be on a beer budget, if you're like most log-home owners we've met, you will muster your pennies, skills, or resources to add something of distinction to your home. It may be a handcrafted front door, fireplace, railing, or porch—or it may simply be colorful window trim or a path that winds through your garden. Big or small, homespun or hired out, those special extras captivate and endear us to the houses we create.

I think of this chapter as a titillating display of special-occasion champagne. There are highlights here from many homes. Some were expensive—just the kind of budget busters we warned you about in chapter one. But before you cry foul, appreciate the fact that owner-builders who save money at the expense of their own labor can sometimes throw caution to the wind at some other point in the building process. In other cases, the owners themselves put their imaginings to paper, then worked them into existence through their own zeal and devotion. Taking on a handcrafted stairway or building a masonry fireplace without prior experience aren't everyday tasks for the faint of heart—nor do they happen without a measure of sacrifice and risk. That they happen at all is testimony to the myriad of families who step out of their comfort zones and into their dreams.

Mostly, these are pictures of ideas—beautiful, practical, whimsical, improbable. Doable or not, you can simply enjoy them. But if by chance a certain picture sets in motion some romantic notion, just maybe you will follow it—all the way *home!*

RIGHT A bentwood railing is a simple but thoughtful addition to this small backyard bridge.

FAR RIGHT When Terry and Sonja Rosenberger learned that it could cost as much as $80,000 to have a craftsman-built waterwheel incorporated into the landscape of their owner-built home, they moved quickly to plan B. Without instructions, Terry drew up a design, then, working by trial and error, fit the 365 carefully sized-and-weighed pieces of his wheel together. The project was completed in two weeks and cost less than $500 in materials.

ABOVE River rock and plaster always work well with logs, but when the masons walked away from this fireplace, something was missing. That's when artist Kim Howard stepped in. Taking her cue from the wallpaper in the dining room, Kim painted a scene reminiscent of old-world Europe.

LEFT Stairways and railings made of wood provide craftsmen endless opportunities to be creative and unique. In this Idaho home, artisan Mike Chase used nature's cursive to weave a "secret" message into his banister.

FAR LEFT Starting with an open sage-covered site, the Thiedes used retired wagons and other abandoned farm memorabilia, along with young trees and fast-growing bushes, to dress up their yard. In the front yard, a second metal-bottomed manure spreader overflows with summer blossoms.

RIGHT The exuberant collaboration of homeowners Liz and Allan Rosen-Ducat with master craftsmen Tim Bullock and Joe Waltman resulted in a house that has a magic all its own. The creative use of twigs, birch bark, and prominent trim harmonize in a multidimensional symphony of texture, color, and form.

BELOW A craftsman can leave his signature in wood as surely as he can on paper. On this Swedish-coped home, scalloped log ends characterize the careful work of a true artist.

ABOVE Antique hardware on handcrafted doors completes a home restoration built with 200-year-old logs.

LEFT With the addition of this kitchen, an early pine cabin is reborn in a new generation. The add-on breaks from the logs with a skillful blend of posts and beams, stone, and stucco.

ABOVE   Oh, how well a home can speak to the fanciful whims, secret fantasies, or desperate hopes of its owner. The late actor Steve McQueen had his Last Chance Ranch built in 1979. Like the rough-and-tumble western films that made him so famous, the cabin speaks to a life with little semblance to offscreen Hollywood. Sadly, Steve died before he ever moved in.

RIGHT   Rustic and simple in theory, the stairway was Steve's idea. It is a single log, halved, then notched with tread.

FAR RIGHT   Today a new family makes their escape from L.A. to this peaceful Idaho retreat where, for just a while, they can take a mental step back into end-of-the-road solitude and the spirit of the Old West.

ABOVE Outside of a two-week log course, Vic Proctor hadn't done much building when he started a family home in Minnesota. As Vic's stairway will attest, "experience is a wonderful teacher!" When the cabin was finished four-and-a-half years later, several friends and neighbors wanted him to build for them. Realizing his special gift, Vic moved his life and family in a new direction to start a career as a log builder.

ABOVE One evening in 1985, Ben Dorn read a how-to-build book from cover to cover. The next day he built his first scriber and finished an advanced book on notch work. On the third day he started the house. Over the next several years he completed his cabin without plans or blueprints. The fireplace, like everything else, is his design, and includes a unique slab of rock shaped like his home state. Ben went on to start a company called Clearwater Log Homes, and to date, he and his crew have completed more than ninety projects.

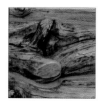

Gary Espe was eighteen and just out of high school when he went off to live alone for four years in the backwoods of Minnesota. His first cabin was a seven-sided log tepee. He learned to build as he went, relying on his own intuition and occasional advice from Norwegian old-timers living near his secluded section of woods. Gary built a spiral staircase, devised his own wooden hinges, and handcrafted all his furniture. He grew a garden, and for meat followed the raven's call to the site of fresh wolf-killed deer. Wizened old Norsemen taught him to cut ice from the river, then keep it stored year-round packed in sawdust in his cellar.

After a time, other people wanted a log tepee like Gary's, and he found himself building again and again. Eventually he started teaching log-building classes at a local community college. Then in

ABOVE This pass-through from dining room to kitchen could have been square, but you may not have stopped to look twice. Now while you're looking, you might also notice the unusual joint securing the timber on the left to the header above. This "seated and curved" variation of a dovetail is Gary's own invention. With a joint like this there's no chance of the timber sheering off under a heavy load.

BELOW The square tenons that secure the treads of this stairway become part of a simple but striking pattern that Gary worked out when he was "playing around." All of Espe's homes are built with green or nearly green logs, and he is forever on a quest for tighter-fitting notches. In the corner of this 1980s home, he used butterfly notches that have two sloping planes as opposed to the saddle notch with only one. More recently, he's switched to yet another technique called over-scribing.

RIGHT Having lived four years as a near recluse, Gary Espe focused his senses on the natural world around him. No doubt his heightened sensitivity contributes to his unique ability to take nature's handiwork and shape it into functional human art. Today he collects and hoards character wood in a makeshift barn fondly referred to as his cathedral. Knowing when and how to peel and store his wood contributes significantly to the beauty of railings like this one.

1979, when he had saved enough money for his own tuition, he went to log-building school in British Columbia. That, he says, opened many new doors, and now, nearly two decades later in Washington State, his world still evolves around the wonders and workings of wood.

ABOVE When Pat and Sheri McNerthney discovered that the 1,000-square-foot octagon they had planned was more house than the two of them could handle, they asked Gary to do the log work. The eight-sided design, with its circular stone chimney and massive walls of glass, was a tricky undertaking in a 2-by-4 world.

LEFT A visitor peering through the McNerthneys' cold entry can appreciate the geometry and detailed craftsmanship in this home, but it didn't happen overnight. Building in spurts, as time and money allowed, the home took nearly twelve years to complete.

FAR LEFT Espe's love for intricate notches and unusual joinery is evident in every cabin he works on. In this home, he describes the support system for the second-floor clerestory and part of the roof as a modified hammer beam—a design that distributes weight through its contributing members. For fun and accent, Gary finishes off his post ends with carvings of various kinds.

ABOVE Burls and knobby bumps generally form as trees cope with parasitic attack. They get bigger as the tree grows but obviously do not weaken the wood or preclude its use in log-house building. James will use them as sparingly or as liberally as his clients' tastes dictate.

Craftsmen are drawn to wood by its warmth, workability, and the boundless opportunities it provides for self-expression. But James Morton, another self-taught artisan who came to a career in log building through the door of his own first home and cabin, is inclined to let the wood speak for itself. Unlike many of his contemporaries, his idea of the perfect house log is most likely to be one that's branched and twisted or profoundly marked by burls, knobs, and cat's eyes.

Starting cautiously at first, he incorporated a single burl into the wall of one of his homes. The owner loved it, along with nearly everyone else who saw it. His next house had more of this distinctive wood, and before long people were clamoring for what James loves to call his "crooked houses." Today he has a small company in Roberts, Montana, aptly named A Very Unique Log Home.

LEFT James sneaks a forked log into a wall, then notches the extra end into the corner so skillfully that you may do a double take. When working his magic, Morton chooses different-sized logs, or shapes them to fit the application. He may use long tapering trunks or trim a twenty-incher down to ten.

ABOVE James takes whatever nature throws his way. Sanded, oiled, and polished, each quirky glitch in the wood becomes a conversation piece in a home.

LEFT The setting sun highlights the sensual curves of oiled and timeworn wood. By comparison, "stain," says James, is a dirty word. While a stained home may require less maintenance, he believes that regular applications of log oil not only make the home look better but extends its life.

For would-be log-home owners who want calluses on their hands but don't have the skills, knowledge, or opportunity to take on the bulk of a house-building project themselves, selecting the right builder may be one of the most important decisions they make. The craftsman who can walk into the lives of a hungry family, adopt their heart's desires, then help them tweak those wants and needs into the "right" home is invaluable.

Retired psychologist Frank Long has been totally blind since the age of sixteen. His wife, Jackie, formerly taught children who others said couldn't learn. Together they make a formidable can-do team, but they were not prepared to take on their retirement home without substantial expert help. Not that they didn't know what they wanted. A box, said Frank. Open. Few walls. No hallways. Tactile and warm, with landmarks as stirring to Frank's non-sighted senses as to Jackie's eyes.

They sat down together over a course of Sundays. Frank designed, Jackie drew. Then they found Thomas Karas—a logsmith with a "touchy-feely portfolio of the odd and unusual." The couple knew instantly that Tom was the person they'd been looking for. Tom took their boxy floor plan, and after trying unsuccessfully to talk them out of a square, set about hiding the fact that it was one. So began a two-year building stint that drew Tom heart and soul into a close-knit, cuss-and-hug relationship that smacked of family and resulted in some of his best work to date.

BELOW Though Frank Long was limited in his ability to share in many tasks, his contribution to the building process may surprise you. Builder Tom Karas has video of him on the business end of a three-pound hammer during log laying. Later he worked with a drawknife, chisel, and hammer, then hand-peeled most of the branches for deck railings and this cedar banister. Jackie Long calls Tom's twig work "noodling." It's part of what makes the house so touchable.

ABOVE A portable band saw is capable of slicing thin sheets of veneer from logs and odd-shaped chunks of wood. When Tom saw one in action, he dragged his own collection of curvy wood to the site for milling. From there he developed a scribe-fit-lamination procedure to create flowing designs on the otherwise plain front door, kitchen cabinets, and drawer fronts. Frank can feel the changing patterns with his fingers, and the couple delights in the different pictures and characters they and their guests find in the wood.

RIGHT The Longs' detached garage is actually stick frame with half-log, white cedar siding. For interest, Tom made a ninety-degree cut down the backside of a whole hand-stripped cedar trunk and fit it on the corner. Thin wood slabs laminated to a standard pre-hung door turned that entryway into something out of the ordinary.

RIGHT Log posts like the ones that frame the moss-rock fireplace and this narrow alcove appear to be lashed together with rope. The effect is purely for aesthetics and is just one of the many extras Carter came up with on the job.

BELOW Not wanting his electric meter on the side of his house, Reverend Agricola opted to put it in full view near his front entry. Then he had Carter wrap up the eyesore in a charming package complete with its own tiny weather vane.

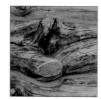

As a small boy, Reverend Hugh Agricola grew up on the very hill where his log house now stands in Gadsden, Alabama. Nearly a lifetime would pass before he would start building, and as Hugh tells it, "My son Jack promised to finish the cabin if the good Lord didn't let me." But the good Lord did. At the age of seventy-five Hugh sat down to draw his first floor-plan rendering. It was fifty feet too long and went through several revisions before he, his son, and Wildwood Log Homes came up with a design that would take another three years to complete.

Much to Hugh's relief, a cancellation at Wildwood substantially shortened the

anticipated two-year waiting period for the log shell. In the meantime, Jack found the man who would take the Agricola cabin from something predictable to the unexpected. His name was Carter Bartlett. Deaf since birth, he came from a large family of competent crafters. Creative, meticulous, and painfully slow, Carter soon ended up moving into the unfinished cabin so he could work all day—and all night too if the mood struck him.

FAR RIGHT Carter was hired as a carpenter, not a mason, but he started with the rock work on the foundation, then moved to the fireplace. Occasionally he'd call on his brothers for help, says Hugh, and he marvels how the whole family seemed to know each other's business. A year passed before Carter laid his hand to wood, but the finished rock work—a unique blend of boulder-size stones with chips and small slices—is pure artistry.

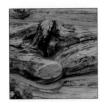

Logs are versatile. Thoughtfully done, a log-home interior can be done up or down to accommodate almost any taste. Even so, tradition is still a powerful driving force behind the architecture of logs. Modified and adapted, the look and feel of the Southwest is a popular theme.

David and Linda Gore's home near Crested Butte, Colorado, is the product of Linda's obsession and a fantastic working relationship with craftsman Steve Cappellucci. More than twenty-eight years back, the Gores started coming from Texas to a log-cabin resort in Colorado. When the retreat came up for sale after fourteen years of visits, they bought it. Another decade passed before they were ready to start a house on land included in their purchase. Work began with another builder, but the relationship was never comfortable. That's when the Gores tracked down Steve. While David mostly worked to pay the bills, Linda threw herself heart and soul into the project. The whole affair was one of the great joys in Linda's life, with the end result being better than anything they had imagined or hoped for. Admiration for Steve's work and mutual respect between both families quickly developed into a lasting friendship. Quips David, "I think, in a bind, I would let Steve take out my appendix!"

LEFT A covered breezeway with vertical poles and decorative posts connects the log garage and guest apartment to the Gores' log-and-stucco home. There was no architect—just Linda and Steve. The overall design is simple and the rooflines uncomplicated. The detail is in the woodwork, says Steve.

BELOW Steve likes action in the roof and the tenacity it takes to put it all together. Powerful and visually striking, the modified hammer-beam trusses spanning the Gores' living room were as fun to build as they were challenging.

LEFT In the Gore home, cabinets, windows, and doors were all custom made by Steve, then dressed and trimmed in hand-peeled pine. Saltillo tiles, white textured walls, and pottery light fixtures complement his distinctly southwestern handiwork.

ABOVE When Fred decided to incorporate old-world Scandinavian-style roofs, he did his homework and talked to owner-builders who had traveled that path before him. Learning from their mistakes, he laid down sod instead of growing it from seed, and waters his high-altitude crop of grass with soaker hoses that run off his regular sprinkler system. Now, he may have to weed his roof, but he can also picnic up there!

Owners who make their living building houses have an advantage in the process of crafting a home for themselves. Even so, new challenges await self-confident builders who will reach farther and higher because they're sure they can. Fred Hibberd has built log houses before—some very nice ones. But when he designed his own house with architect Kristoffer Prestrude, he incorporated some longed-for yet very experimental features, including sod roofs and an indoor sprinkler system designed to automatically water plants in out-of-reach places.

LEFT The kitchen spills into the large bay overlooking the Hibberds' carefully tended garden—a literal smorgasbord of wildflowers and native grasses with just enough lawn to tickle your toes.

BELOW As a builder living near the upscale resort town of Jackson Hole, Wyoming, Fred Hibberd has listened to log-home owners pine for cozy spaces, then watched them build massive homes where the only intimate space is in the closet! In his design, modest living spaces are neatly separated. Here, the family room measures only 16 by 14 feet. The fireplace and rock wall, Southwest latilla ceiling, and window-seat nook are all expensive features that become more manageable when done on a smaller scale.

ABOVE Put-your-boots-up furnishings bid you to come and sit a spell on this tranquil front porch.

Your land is the beginning place. You cannot properly design your home until you know the site—where the views are, how the sun will rise and set, local traffic patterns, and so on. If you can observe your land through the seasons, all the better. Picnic there, pitch a tent, have coffee with the neighbors. Then stake your claim and put the natural elements to work, integrating them into the way you want to live. Add-on spaces such as decks and porches will be part of the process. They are architecturally pleasing in their own right, but you will enjoy those spaces more if you design them with real use in mind.

ABOVE Front-porch chats and late-night suppers are a birthright in the humid South. So are pesky mosquitos. Refusing to be carried off by bugs, the Lauderdales screened off a section of their wraparound porch.

RIGHT When Bob and Franz Kudelski moved from Florida's summer swelter to the mountain cool of Montana, they spent days on their property siting the house and thinking up ways to make the most of their location. A hot tub sunk into their spacious, view-conscious deck is pleasant assurance that they can enjoy this outdoor living area year-round.

RIGHT When Arthur and Sarah Peters started coming to their Wyoming ranch more than fifty years ago, nine days of their two-week vacation were spent driving from New York. They lived in an ancient two-room cabin without running water or electricity and bathed their children in the irrigation ditch out back. They've been back every year since, but it wasn't until 1989 that they built a larger, updated cabin to accommodate the overflow of family and friends. First designed in fits of inspiration on the back of market lists, the new cabin was simple and practical. Their screened porch is a welcome respite from the bugs, a peaceful retreat for working and writing, an on and off stopover for outdoor gear, and convenient storage for winter's wood. If only it were bigger!

6 DESIGN & CONSTRUCTION
OF A SMALL LOG BUILDING—ART THIEDE

As a log-home builder for the past sixteen years, I have seen an incredible transformation take place in log-home construction. I hope our previous books had some influence on this renaissance in logs. They presented an awesome display of log-home architecture that was pretty lavish, showing how far log-home design has come from its pioneer roots. With this book, we return to those roots somewhat. In this chapter we explore our log-building heritage through the building and design of a simple log structure.

My interest in log homes began when I was about ten years old. Living in New York City and hating every minute of it, my imagination went berserk upon receiving my first Lincoln Log set. Through those pre-notched brown logs I was able to escape the dreariness and oppression of the city and fantasize my way to the American frontier, where I assumed everybody lived in log cabins. Unfortunately, it took me another twenty years to turn my fantasy into reality. In 1980 my best friend, Mike Hautzenroder, and I went to Prince George, British Columbia, to attend the B. Allan Mackie School of Log Building. I had just received a commission to rebuild a historic log structure in our community of Tahoe City, California, that had recently burned down. Realizing that my childhood building experience wouldn't cut it for this project, we headed north to learn from the master himself.

My days at Mackie's school were some of the most memorable of my life. For six weeks we ate, slept, and talked log building. I became extremely proficient with

tools that I had never used before in my life. Chain saws, scribers, axes, drawknives, blocks and tackles, etc., were everyday tools of the trade. While most of our fellow students chose chain saws for carving their saddle notches, Mike and I used axes. We would get up extra early in the morning so we could practice before the regular classes began. After several weeks we could hew out a notch as fast as anybody with a chain saw. The chips flew out of those frozen logs like shrapnel from a bomb. Swing after swing the axe head came down into the log, wafer-close to the scribe line without ever (well hardly ever) missing the mark. No screaming chain saw, spilled oil and gas, or fumes. Just a log, an axe, and the determination to get it done—the very essence of building with logs.

Along with learning how to build with logs there was another equally important facet to Mackie's school: we all experienced the joys of living in a log cabin. Each class built a small cabin as their log-building project, and these cabins were then used by succeeding classes. The school was about thirty miles from the nearest town and was located in pretty much a wilderness area. There were no phones, running water, gas, or electricity to the cabins. We cooked our food on a woodstove that also provided our heat. We melted snow for water, read by the light of Aladdin lamps, and went to town once a week to shower, get supplies, and wash our clothes. It was a fairly rustic living experience, especially in the dead of winter with the daily high around 5 degrees Fahrenheit.

So, three of us lived in this 20-by-20-foot cabin for six weeks while we attended the school. By today's standards this cabin was somewhat primitive, but to us it was pretty deluxe. It was our first log-home living experience, and as I sit here at the computer some eighteen years later—reminiscing and getting more nostalgic by the sentence—I realize that, like hewing those notches with an axe, this was the essence of "living the log-cabin experience." Even though I have photographed, built, and lived in far grander log homes, including the one we live in now, it never got any better than that.

Now, you may be saying to yourself, "Sure, living in 400 square feet for six weeks is one thing, but could you do it with a family of four?" Probably not, but I know one thing for sure—that we could live in less space than we have now, and that, I believe, is the key to building small: knowing and accepting the fact that you can live just as well, maybe better, in smaller spaces.

So, with that mind-set, I would like to take you through the design and construction of this simple, small log structure. From time to time I will deviate from the project at hand to discuss other options in building and design. Most of these digressions will be directed towards building more efficiently. As we progress through the different phases of this project, keep in mind that we are discussing building and design in very general terms. This is not a building manual. Look to this chapter as a representation of a small log structure and how it evolved from design to finish, why we made the decisions we did, and what the alternatives were. We present new ideas here and some refreshing perspectives on old ones.

The building we used for illustration purposes is a horse barn that I constructed recently. Of course, there are

ABOVE Built as a horse barn, this structure could have just as easily been designed as a small cabin. It took about one month to build, using three-sided logs milled by the author.

differences between a barn and a house, but many of the building elements are common to both. With additional thought given to electrical, heating, and plumbing systems, this structure could very well serve as a small cabin. In fact, this design, with a central pass-through, was very common east of the Mississippi during the last century and was known affectionately as the "dog trot cabin" (see *American Log Homes,* p. 62).

Build It on Paper

The construction of a building, big or small, should always start with a well-thought-out plan. Budget, use, site, and environment are some of the factors that influence the design, whether it is built of logs, adobe, or marshmallows. At the heart of a building plan is the floor plan. If building small is our goal, then we need to ensure that this objective is our top priority. In the case of the horse barn, cost was a major consideration and, of course, this affected size. The owners of the property had previously contracted with an architect for a barn design that turned out to be very handsome but very expensive. As often happens, dreams obscured the reality of building costs, and the result was a plan that was unworkable. That in itself might not have been so bad except that several thousands of dollars had been spent before this was realized. So now the budget was tightened even further. Is there a lesson to be learned here? You bet there is! If you are like most, you are building to a budget. Don't let dreams of grandeur cloud your focus. Design for expansion, not extravagance.

I sat down with the clients and discussed their needs. I then built a scale model of the proposed structure out of quarter-inch foam board. Even though this was a simple design, a model helped the clients understand the spatial relationships of the structure. It took just a few hours to produce and ensured that there would be fewer misunderstandings between builder and client. The resultant plan encompassed a total of 912 square feet under roof, with 576 of those within the log walls.

After the conceptual plan had been developed and approved by the client, it was time to generate the working drawings for submission to the building department for a construction permit. Since this was a simple structure with an engineered truss roof (more on trussed roofs later), I drew up the plans myself. I have a pretty good working relationship with the building inspector and had little trouble getting my permit. If you don't have this kind of relationship, you may have to get an architect and/or structural engineer to draw your plans. In any case, "Decoding Building Codes" is an Internet resource I heartily recommend reading. It gives valuable insight into this important area that is especially relevant to log homes.

God's Half Acre

All the buildings that were ever built have one thing in common: they rest on a piece of earth called the building site. In this particular case there was not much latitude in determining where this site would be. An existing house and building setbacks from property lines pretty much dictated where it was to be placed. However, if this were a cabin on an undeveloped piece of land, there would be many considerations in this regard.

Since discussion of all the criteria that influence the selection process for land are beyond the scope of this chapter, we would refer you to the resource directory for that information. However, one criterion that is very relevant to small-house design is site selection in regard to basements, especially of the daylight variety. Keep in mind that if you want to have a daylight basement you need to have a building site that has some grade (slope) to it. How much slope you need depends in part on the size and design of the house, but typically from three to eight feet across the building envelope is sufficient. If there is little or no slope to the property, you can still have a basement, but it will probably not be of the daylight or walkout kind. Other considerations in basement design are the topography and soil conditions. If in doubt as to whether the site is suitable for a basement, contact a hydrologist or soils engineer. Better to have no basement than a wet one!

Down in the Ground

There is a similarity between sewage systems, water supply systems, and foundations. They are out of sight and therefore out of mind, for the most part. You flush the toilet, turn on the faucet, and just take for granted that the house is anchored securely to the ground. Nothing here to get excited about. Nothing, that is, unless you view the foundation as something more than just a support and anchor for the house.

When it came time to design the foundation system for the horse barn, two decisions influenced what system we used: for the tack-and-feed part of the barn, the client wanted a concrete slab floor; for the stall part, a gravel floor was indicated. Therefore, for the tack/feed part of the structure a standard footing-and-stem-wall foundation was built. This facilitated pouring and finishing a slab within the foundation walls for the floor. This same foundation system could have been used for the stall section of the barn, but I decided to use a post-and-pier foundation here to save on building costs. Since a continuous seal between the lowest course of logs and ground was not important, this worked just fine. We

An Alternative Foundation

As building costs escalate, I am constantly looking for ways to build for less money without sacrificing function, comfort, or structural integrity. In understanding the following system, bear in mind that it combines the functions of a foundation, structural floor, finished floor, and heating system into one entity, thus saving some costs.

The heart of this system is the "frost-protected shallow foundation." This can be a very cost-effective design, especially in climates where the foundation footings must go deep in order to get below the frost line. In a typical footing-and-stem-wall foundation system such as we used on part of the barn, the footings needed to be placed about three feet below natural grade in order to protect the foundation from frost-heaving. In more northern latitudes than our own (southern Idaho), expect four- and five-foot depths. This requires a lot of excavation and concrete to bring the wall back above grade. Since this is more foundation than is needed to support the building, if we can find another means to protect against frost-heave we can reduce foundation costs. The trick here is to use geothermal heat from within the earth and heat loss from within the building to raise the frost depth to a level that will permit a slab-on-grade (or below) type of foundation. This is accomplished through careful placement of underground insulation, and can raise the footing depth to as little as sixteen inches in even the most severe climates.

As shown in the illustration, this system employs a concrete slab that is thickened at its perimeter to support the wall loads. This thickened section, in effect, becomes a grade beam. Both the slab and beam can be formed together and poured monolithically, saving on labor and material. By incorporating hydronic radiant heat within the slab and finishing the slab by acid etching,

imprinting, coloring, or any combination of these techniques, we have a foundation, floor, and heating system in place. Sound too good to be true? Well, if you have the right soil conditions, good drainage, and understanding code officials, this is a most viable approach to cutting building costs. Remember, though, that because the frost-protected shallow-foundation system is relatively new to this country, one must carefully assess its acceptance by local code officials before expending time and effort in this direction.

In addition to the above foundation detail, an all-weather wood foundation wall system can also be employed for basement applications. The advantages of this technology are:

1. It enables a builder (possibly yourself) without concrete or block foundation experience to complete the foundation.
2. It creates a more receptive wall for plumbing, electrical, and insulating needs than concrete does.

To summarize here, we need to realize once again that a well-executed building plan is absolutely essential. Drainage, both above and below grade, needs to be dealt with effectively. Partition walls on the concrete slab (which may need to buttress the foundation walls) need to be defined and adhered to so that there is no conflict with hydronic lines. Electrical and plumbing routes need to be established, since some of them will be coming through the slab. Insulation, vapor barrier, and radon issues need to be addressed, especially in basement designs. Compared to the more common stem-wall foundation with its attendant crawl space, the slab-on-grade foundation system demands more detailed and thorough planning. But if reducing building costs is your priority, then this system is definitely worth considering.

This illustration shows how much more excavation and concrete it takes to construct a conventional foundation as opposed to a frost-protected shallow foundation. Combined with a slab on grade and hydronic heating within the slab, a substantial amount of money can be saved over more conventional crawl-space construction.

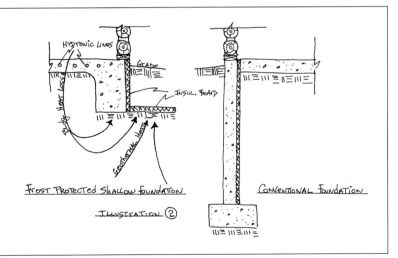

ABOVE The author used a band-saw mill to dimension all the logs to a seven-inch thickness. This made for an easy "stack" of the walls with no notching at the corners. The mill is portable so it can be trailered to the job site or to the woods, whichever is the more convenient location for milling.

ABOVE RIGHT With a butt-and-pass system, the corners of this building were very simple to erect. There wasn't a need to notch the logs, just to square-cut the ends. This was possible because of the three-sided log profile.

RIGHT Every morning, like clockwork, this blue grouse flew in from the nearby woods to check on our progress. We made him a member of the crew and paid him with scraps from our lunches.

LOWER RIGHT Waxing the twelve-inch spikes made driving them into the undersized holes much easier.

just had to make sure the tops of the piers in the stall area matched the elevation of the foundation in the tack area. This was important so that as the two separate wall sections grew, they matched where they came together, about twelve courses up from the foundation.

"Logitecture"

Initially, the barn client did not have a preference to building style or design. It wasn't imperative that the structure be built of logs. After tossing around frame, post-and-beam, and various log designs, I decided that using three-sided milled logs for the structure would be the most cost-effective and expedient method of construction. The reasons for this are as follows:

1. Possibly the most important reason for choosing a three-sided log was the fact that I have my own sawmill for processing the logs. This not only holds down the cost of milling but also permits using a lower and less-expensive grade of log than you would need in other types of log construction. (By lower grade, I don't mean an inferior log but one in which lack of straightness and taper are of less concern.) Of course, not everybody has his own sawmill, but chances are there is someone not too far away with a portable mill like mine who would come to your site to mill your logs.

2. The second most important reason for using this style of log in the stack is the ease of corner detail using the butt-and-pass method of log joinery. This barn of simple design still had eight corners to every course, but this style of corner connection is about as simple as they come. No scribing or notching is required, just

a simple square cut at the end of the log that butts into the cross log of the adjoining wall.

This butt-and-pass method of log joinery does have one drawback: because it is not a true notch it doesn't create a weather-tight seal against air infiltration. This was not a problem with the barn, but if I were to use this connection on a cabin or house, I would have to use caulking, gasketing, or splining, or create a simple notch of one log into the other. This particular choice of notch is a good example of matching the log work to the use of the building. It took us less than a week to stack the log walls for this barn, whereas it might have taken three times that long if we had used some sort of scribed notch.

3. Another advantage in using a milled log for this type of structure is the ease in which one is able to reinforce the walls around door and window openings. One of the important aspects of building with logs is the necessity of restoring structural rigidity to the wall after cutting out window and door openings. There are many ways of doing this, the simplest being to lag-screw a vertical member next to the opening. By connecting the cut logs with the sill log and header log (bottom and top of opening), strength is returned to the wall with a minimum expenditure of labor and materials.

4. One final advantage in using a milled log as opposed to a round log is that the flat surface of the log is both easier to fasten to the foundation and easier to frame a roof to. This translates to less labor and less costs.

To summarize, the choice of using a sawn log in this design meant reduced labor costs, both in time and in the use of

relatively unskilled labor. Material costs were also reduced because we were able to use a less-expensive log than round-log design would have required. There were milling costs, to be sure, but even these were mitigated by the fact that we had less of the log to peel once we milled three sides of it. Some of the log-slab cutoffs were even used as trim, and the rest were recycled into firewood. All in all, I felt pretty good about using the most appropriate log style for this building, especially given the budget constraints.

Up with the Logs

In our travels throughout the U.S. and Canada, we have seen many differ-

ABOVE To restore rigidity to the wall after we cut out door and window openings, we lagged these 4-by-4 strongbacks into each side of the opening.

ent styles of log buildings. For the most part, these styles can be broken down into two main groups: the notched-log structure and the posted-log structure, with its hybrids. There is another style of log work called the palisade, or vertical log, but this style is pretty much relegated to historical buildings or is sometimes used as a decorative element on a horizontal log

ABOVE We added a bit of log detailing here, utilizing the log cutoffs from the milling process.

RIGHT There are many interesting log details in this photograph of the Chief Joseph Ranch. Of particular interest is the creative use of vertical logs above the window.

BELOW Using a chain saw to cut the seven-inch logs made quick work of this phase of construction. We then used a four-inch grinder to true up the cut.

ABOVE Getting an accurate cut line on the logs was easy, as there were three flat sides from which to work.

structure, especially on the gable ends. Although I was schooled in the notched style of building, it didn't take me long to realize the advantages of building in the posted style with both round and sawn logs. In fact, most of the log structures that I have built over the past ten years, except the horse barn, have been of this construction, which the French refer to as *piece en piece*.

The advantages of posted-log construction over notched-log building are primarily economic. By substituting a log post for the notches at a building corner, there is a substantial savings in labor costs. Another advantage of posted-log construction that the early settlers of our country certainly recognized is the ability to use short logs to create long walls. Shorter logs are always easier to come by and they are easier to get up on the walls. So, the question is, "If posted-log construction is cheaper and easier than notched-log building, why didn't we use that style for the horse barn?" Actually, we did consider using posted corners but decided against it for two reasons:

1. The butt-and-pass method of log joinery used on the barn was actually less labor intensive than using a post. There really isn't any notch work, just a square cut on the end of the log where it butts to the log on the opposing wall.

2. The pier foundation in the stall area of the barn precluded the use of posts, as there wasn't enough bearing area on the concrete columns to accept both the post and wall log.

Building with logs is typically more labor intensive than conventional frame construction. By choosing your log style carefully, you can effect considerable savings on this labor, as we did on the barn. While a full round log with saddle-notched corners might have been more aesthetically pleasing, the higher labor costs associated with this system would have doomed the project from the start. So don't just assume that all log buildings are created equal. Research the options and choose the most economical style that will suit your needs.

Let There Be Light

A significant part of building a log structure involves cutting out the door and window openings. This can be accomplished in a variety of ways. I will explain what I have found to be the easiest and most expedient method.

If you are building on-site (as we did on the barn project), you can cut the finished openings just before the header log (that is, the first continuous log across the opening) goes down. This permits you to bring the chain saw into the cut from directly above the cut line. If the opening goes into the header log (as it probably will), this part of the cut can be completed on the header log while it is on the ground. This is much easier than cutting it on the wall after the log is in place.

The actual cut should be made using a sharp chain that can cruise through the

logs. Your chain saw should be powerful enough to maintain the high rpm's necessary to make a smooth straight cut through all the logs without bogging down.

There are some cutting jigs available that supposedly let even a novice make a straight cut, but I prefer to do this freehand so as to save time. The trick lies not in making the actual cut but in getting a good, visible plumb line down the face of the logs that can be seen when the sawdust is flying. If you have left a few extra inches of log past your final cut lines, you can always take a couple of practice cuts. If this doesn't work, then there's the option of going to the next size window or door unit.

Since an opening in a log wall compromises the structural integrity of the wall, a means must be found to restore rigidity to this area. In the barn we did this, as mentioned previously, by lag-screwing a 4-by-4 post into the logs on both sides of the opening. This 4-by-4 runs from the sill-plate log to the rafter-plate log, thus effectively tying the weaker cut logs to the stronger through logs. However, in a house design you may not want the intrusion of these "strong back posts," so another means must be found through an intersecting interior or exterior wall, or through the rough framing of the opening itself. Various books on log building present other options.

BELOW Cutting the door and window openings calls for a sharp chain and an equally sharp mind. A screw-up here can make for a real "bad hair day."

Through the Roof

There is a building axiom that states "the more square footage you incorporate under a roof of fixed dimensions, the cheaper that space becomes." This is usually the case, because the roof can be the single most expensive building component in the structure. If this is true, then it would be an area where the builder and designer really need to come to grips with costs.

I have seen roofs finished with slate, flashed with copper, and framed with logs. Some have enough angles, planes, and pitches to keep the best roof cutter awake at night. A roof such as this could easily cost as much as it would to build an entire house for most of us. Questions the cost-conscious builder/designer must ask are: "How can I design a roof that will minimize materials (especially expensive ones) and minimize labor (using factory-built trusses for example)? How can I keep the design simple and functional to both minimize labor costs and maximize performance?" (Many times a complex roof design will not perform well in cold climates because of heat loss resulting in ice damming. It is true that these heat-loss problems can be mitigated with roof venting, extra insulation, etc., but at what cost?)

Most of the log houses that I build now use a factory-supplied truss or site-built truss as the main structural component because of the inherent cost savings in such a design. To keep the structure from having a "low income housing" look, I incorporate detailing that spices up the design (more on that later).

While trusses can be a viable alternative to custom-framed roofs, there is another system that may be even more cost effective, though I have not personally used it yet. That system uses the stressed-skin insulated panel as its primary structural component. In a way, these insulated panels mimic a log wall in performance. They integrate structure, finish, and insulation into a single module, greatly simplifying the building process. They come in a variety of "sandwiches," utilizing different thicknesses of insulation and different skins. These skins can be structural bases or finished treatments. (See AFM Corporation in the resource directory.) While there are some trade-offs that need to be considered with such a system (the panels work best with simple roof designs that mini-mize roof cuts for valleys, dormers, split-roof pitches, etc.), the savings in building costs can be substantial.

So, if that log dream home just came in at twice what you can afford, look to the roof as a way to bring costs back to earth. In fact, before you look at the roof you should look at the floor plan that the roof has to cover. That is where the simplification really begins.

It's in the Details

Throughout this chapter there has been a recurring theme of cost-effective design and building. That is partially what this book is all about. So, it is with some guilt that I present this section on detailing, because it is something that you can really do without. Detailing (done thoughtfully) can actually save you money. That sounds like a contradiction, but let me explain.

Nobody, or almost nobody, wants to live in a home that is so bland, so devoid of interest and charm that it resembles a Quonset hut. (You know, that metal building the government erected by the tens of thousands during and after WWII that resembled a giant culvert. In fact, I think they *were* giant culverts!) After all, one of the reasons many people choose to live in log homes is because, by the very nature of their construction, they tend not to be "cookie cutter" examples of the building trade. How do you make your home unique without breaking the bank? In the details.

We spoke previously about how expensive some roof systems can be, especially if they are framed with logs. The same is true for most parts of a building constructed of logs. While log walls themselves are cost effective because of the multiplicity of uses that the logs fulfill (structural, insulative, exterior and interior finish, etc.) the same cannot be said for other applications of logs within the structure. For example, a floor system framed with logs is going to cost more than one framed in dimensioned lumber. The roof is certainly going to cost more in logs, especially if engineering requires additional structure beyond the logs themselves (very common, especially in high snow-load areas). Other design elements in a building, such as dormers, bays or pop-outs, stairs, etc., can also be cost prohibitive in a conservative building budget if framed in logs.

The trick is to frame these items in conventional lumber and then add log detailing so they appear to have been built with logs. For example, false log rafters could be applied to the underside of a roof to give the impression that logs indeed were used in the framework. Corner posts and log-slab siding could be applied to a conventionally framed dormer to give the same effect. Log posts can be scattered throughout the building in both structural and nonstructural applications from the entry to the living room. (This is a popular way of adding log accents to both log and non-log structures, because where logs might not be suitable for structural applications such as girders, beams, and rafters, they are more than adequate for posts.) Even exterior roof projections like ridges, purlins, and rafter tails can be "dummied" in to provide the illusion of a roof structure built in logs. (Refer to *The Log Home Book,* pages 195–96, for more on this.)

So, get creative! The simple use of log slabs that were left over from milling the logs for the barn not only breaks up the empty space in the gable ends but serves as a visual tie between the roof, which has no logs, and the walls, which do. If the budget would have allowed, I could have applied log accents to simulate a ridge and purlins as described above.

There are, of course, many places in a building where log details can be applied effectively. Though we have described just a few of the possibilities, if one looks carefully at the pictures within this book many more opportunities present themselves. From window and door trim to railings, posts, knee braces, fireplace mantels, log-slab siding in both horizontal and vertical applications, the list goes on and on. But be careful, because too much detailing in this regard can begin to look busy, too contrived. Keep it simple, well-crafted, and in proportion to the rest of the building. The results will speak for themselves.

I hope that by reading this you gained some insight into log building and design that perhaps you hadn't known of. It can be tough to build small because our attitudes and expectations have been conditioned in the other direction for so long. As I look to our next log-house design, I won't forget the first one I lived in. It was only 400 square feet but had a warmth and coziness to it that speaks to me still. It also had a Styrofoam toilet seat in the outhouse that made it all work on those below-zero nights, if you know what I mean.

Bibliography

Design Guide for Frost-Protected Shallow Foundations. Washington, D.C.: The National Association of Homebuilders, 1995.

Fine Homebuilding 74, (May 1992): 104.

7 RESOURCE DIRECTORY

Builders of Log Homes

Abbey, Steve: P.O. Box 55, Howe, Idaho 83244, (208) 767-3366. Restorations and recycled log homes: will build or consult. (See Abbey house, p. 75.)

Alpine Log Homes: P.O. Box 85, Victor, Montana 59875, (406) 642-3451. Design and construction of full-round, handcrafted log homes. (See Farley house, p. 32.)

Big Timberworks, Inc.: P.O. Box 368, Gallatin Gateway, Montana 59730, (406) 763-4639. Specializes in timber-frame design and construction using all recycled materials. (Big Timberworks provided the timber-frame trusses for the Macleans' house, see p. 36.)

Blue Mountain Builders: Noah Bradley, P.O. Box 196, Wolftown, Virginia 22748, (540) 948-5258. Log cabin restorations, stonework, and timber frame. (See Craig house, p. 112; Virginia Family cabin, p. 116; Altaffer house, p. 124.)

Bullock and Company, Master Craftsmen: P.O. Box 275, Creemore, Ontario, Canada L0M 1G0, (705) 466-2505, Fax (705) 466-3577. Designers, builders, and consultants of handcrafted log and timber structures. (See Rosen-Ducat house, pp. 148, 149.)

Cappellucci, Steve: 635 County Rd., #744, Almont, Colorado 81210, (970) 641-3367. Design and construction of handcrafted log homes, cabinetry, and furniture. (See pp. 168–69.)

Clearwater Log Homes: Ben Dorn, P.O. Box 391, Hayden Lake, Idaho 83835, (208) 772-7891. Handcrafted, full-scribe log homes. (See p. 155.)

Custom Log Homes: P.O. Drawer 218, Stevensville, Montana 59870, (406) 777-5202, Fax (406) 777-2738. Design and construction of hand-hewn, full-round chinked, Swedish-coped, and post-and-beam log homes. (See Kudelski house, pp. 18, 19, 174–75.)

Edens Construction: Steve Edens, 308 Sheafman Creek Rd., Victor, Montana 59875, (406) 961-3606. Handcrafted log homes and traditional frame construction. (See Kudelski house, pp. 18, 19.)

Espe, Gary: Norwegian Wood Log Homes, 18920 River Rd., Leavenworth, Washington 98826, (509) 763-3675. Handcrafted, full-scribe log and timber-frame homes, railings, furniture, and unique wood carvings. (See pp. 156–59.)

Hearthstone Log Homes: 1630 East Hwy 25-70, Dandridge, Tennessee 37725, (423) 397-9425 or (1-800) 247-4442. Custom designs, hand-hewn and machine-worked logs, dovetail joinery, and timber-frame construction. (See p. 17.)

Hibberd, Fred: Timberline Corporation, 400 NW Ridge Rd., Jackson, Wyoming 83001, (307) 733-7327. Custom, round-log homes. (See pp. 170–71.)

Interlochen Log & Timber: U.S. 31 S., Interlochen, Michigan 49643, (616) 275-3400.

Karas, Thomas: P.O. Box 368 and 4715 Bush Rd., Interlochen, Michigan 49643, (616) 276-5178. Custom-milled log homes, cabinetry, and furnishings with uncommon artistic flare. (See pp. 164–65.)

Logcrafters: Mary and Stuart Thompson, P.O. Box 1540, Pinedale, Wyoming 82941, (307) 367-2502, Fax (307) 367-4475. Uses a variety of log construction techniques but specializes in super-efficient "sandwich wall" construction. (See Thompson house, pp. 128–33.)

McRaven, Charles: Charles McRaven Restorations, Drawer G, Free Union, Virginia 22940, (804) 973-4859. Hewn log homes, post and beam, restorations, stone masonry, hand-split rails, and blacksmithing. (See Stein house, pp. 120–23, 150–51, 172.)

Morton, James: A Very Unique Log Home, P.O. Box 2052, Red Lodge, Montana 59068, (406) 446-2406. Handcrafted, Swedish-coped log homes chock-full of burls, cat's-eyes, and knobbies. (See pp. 160–63.)

Mayers, Randell: Westbank Construction, Inc., Box 527, Teton Village, Wyoming 83025, (307) 733-9286. Handcrafted, full-round, chinked log homes. (See pp. 14, 15.)

Muth, Trip: Muth Carpentry, 1302 Hawk Mountain Rd., Kempton, Pennsylvania 19529. (See p. 111.)

Pederson, Jeff: P.O. Box 788, Challis, Idaho 83226, (208) 879-4211. Traditional hand-hewn log homes (See Maclean house, pp. 36–41.)

Platt, Criss: CRS Construction, 750 Eldorado Ave. E.S.R., Nederland, Colorado 80466, (303) 494-1908, Fax (303) 494-3498. Custom homes: log and other. (See Baby Bear cabin, pp. 134–37.)

Prendergast, Tony: Box 103, Crestone, Colorado 81131, (719) 256-4471. Specializes in alternative and earth-friendly construction with logs, stone, adobe, straw bale, earth berm, recycled tires, and more. (See Prendergast-Kane house, pp. 52–55.)

Proctor, Vic: Vic Proctor Log Homes, 2828 Esterbrook Rd., Douglas, Wyoming 82633, (307) 351-1765. Handcrafted, full-round, chinked, or scribed log homes. (See p. 154.)

Rocky Mountain Log Homes: 1883 Hwy 93 S., Hamilton, Montana 59840, (406) 363-5680. Custom-designed milled and log-frame homes. For a handcrafted home, contact Rocky Mountain's sister company, **Pioneer Log Homes:** 1344 Hwy 93, Victor, Montana 59875, (406) 961-3273. (See Phelps house, pp. 42–45.)

Shelter Associates Ltd.: 4235 Free Union Rd., Free Union, Virginia 22940, (804) 973-8307. Specializing in estate restorations and the design and construction of custom homes. (See pp. 150, 151, 172.)

Stegman, Steven: Quantum Construction Co., 245 Starr Rd., Otego, New York 13825, (607) 988-9110. Designs and builds custom homes. (See Stegman house, pp. 103–07.)

Stopal, Richard "Log Home": P.O. Box 1281, Hailey, Idaho 83333, (208) 788-9693. Custom, handcrafted log homes, all styles of construction.

Thiede, Art: Woody's Log Homes and Crane Service, P.O. Box 2735, Hailey, Idaho 83333, (208) 788-4393, e-mail: thiede@ sunvalley.net. Handcrafted, full-round, or sawn-log homes. (See pp. 56–65.)

Thomas Wood Handcrafted Log Homes: P.O. Box 772418, Steamboat Springs, Colorado 80477, (970) 879-3935. Handcrafted, full-round, scribed-log homes. (See Ericksen-Bush house, pp. 28–31.)

Timmerhus, Inc.: Ed Shure, 3000 N. 63rd St., Boulder, Colorado 80301, (303) 449-1336, Fax (303) 449-9170. Designs and builds handcrafted, scribe-fit log homes and timber-frame structures. Also doors, windows, cabinets. (See Baby Bear cabin, pp. 134–37.)

Waltman and Company: Joe Waltman, 59 Marina Rd., Yarmouth, Maine 04096, (207) 846-3810, Fax (207) 846-6192. Custom designed and built log and traditional framed homes. (See Rosen-Ducat house, pp. 148, 149.)

Wildwood Handcrafted Log Homes: P.O. Box 1365, Pigeon Forge, Tennessee 37868-1365, (423) 428-1932, Fax (423) 428-3384. Traditional, hand-hewn log homes. (See Agricola house, pp. 166–67.)

Architects and Designers

Carney, Nancy and John: Carney Architects, P.O. Box 9218, Jackson, Wyoming 83002 (307) 733-5546. (See Peters' porch, p. 174-175.)

Gassman, Michael: Architect, P.O. Box 740, Aspen, Colorado, 81612, (970) 925-2695. (See Baby Bear cabin, pp. 134–37.)

Knudson Gloss Architects: John Knudson, 4820 Riverbend Rd., Boulder, Colorado 80301, (303) 442-5882.

Prestrude, Kristoffer, AIA: Prestrude Architect, P.O. Box 3624, Jackson, Wyoming 83001, (307) 733-5391. (See Hibberd, pp. 170–71.)

Steinbrecher, Jean: Architect. P.O. Box 788, Langley, Washington 98260-0788, (360) 221-0494.

Antiques, Reproductions, and Other Stuff

AFM Corporation: 24000 W. Hwy 7, Suite 201, Excelsior, Minnesota 55331, (612) 474-0809. Source for stressed-skin insulated panels.

Chusie Mountain Interiors: Chuck and Susie Robbins, P.O. Box 1579, 59000 N. Hwy 69, Westcliffe, Colorado 81252, (719) 783-9608. (See Fulton house, pp. 80–85.)

Jim Croft, Sunrise Productions: Box 194, Boyd, Montana 49013, (1-800) 843-3607. Log-home book and resource center. URL: sunrise-productions.com.

Incinolet Toilet Research Products/ Blankenship: 2639 Andjon, Dallas, Texas 75220, (1-800) 527-5551. The Incinolet toilet electrically incinerates human waste to a germ-free ash. Needs no septic; installs like a clothes dryer.

Light Years Antiques: Mike Dalio, Arvada, Colorado 80002, (303) 422-4379. By appointment only. Antique, reproduction, and custom-crafted light fixtures; also repairs and plates. (See Fulton house, pp. 80–85.)

Roof shakes and aging solution for wood: Jim and Nancy Carey, The Cedar Guild, P.O. Box 249, Lyons, Oregon 97358, (1-800) 270-2541, Fax (503) 897-2442, e-mail: cedarinfo!cedar-guild.com. Custom cedar roof and sidewall shakes and Victorian-pattern shingles. URL:http:/www.cedar-guild.com.

Silent refrigerator by Electrolux: The refrigerator referred to on page 136 has an electrically heated absorption cooling unit that is virtually silent in operation. Manufactured by Electrolux and purchased at Peter Jones (department store) Export Department, Sloane Square, London, England SW1W 8EL, (011-44-171) 730-3434. Also available through Peter Jones: miniature dishwasher by Bosch (240 volt), model SKT20.

Snelling's Thermo-Vac Inc.: P.O. Box 210, Blanchard, Louisiana 71009, (318) 929-7398, Fax (318) 929-3923. High-quality, formed-plastic ceiling tiles designed to mimic old tin. (See Fulton house, pp. 82–85.)

Thorpe, Tom: 11026 Elk Run Rd., Catlett, Virginia 20119, (540) 788-9911. Will locate, salvage, and move old log cabins and plantation homes. (See pp. 125–26.)

Woodmizer Products: 8180 W. 10th St., Indianapolis, Indiana 46214, (1-800) 553-0182, URL: http://www.woodmizer. com/ sawmill.htm. (See Thiede farmhouse, pp. 60-65.) Manufacturer of the Woodmizer portable sawmill. Also contact for information on mill owners and operators in the U.S.

Artisans, Furniture Makers, and Interior Decorators

Art on Anything: Jeri VanDeusen, 11989 E. Yale Ave., Aurora, Colorado 80014, (303) 755-1651. Hand-painted tiles, fixtures, trompe l'oeil, faux.

Bartlett, Carter: 2504 Walnut St., Albertville, Alabama 35950, (205) 891-2983. (See pp. 166–67.)

By Design Interiors, Inc.: Susie Moreland, 623 S. 1st St., Hamilton, Montana 59840, (406) 363-4473, Fax (406) 363-1877. (See Kudelski interiors, pp. 18, 19.)

Chase, Mike: Chase Construction, P.O. Box 3910, Ketchum, Idaho 83340, (208) 788-2379. Handcrafted log homes, unique railings, and furniture. (See stairway, p. 147.)

Evans, Rich: Ketchum Kustom Woodworks, Inc., P.O. Box 1448, Ketchum, Idaho 83340, (208) 726-1905, Fax (208) 726-1277. (See Cole kitchen, p. 73.)

Gladfelter, Todd: RD2, Box 71-B3, New Ringgold, Pennsylvania 17960. (717) 943-2198. Fine Furniture. (See Gladfelter-Ross house, pp. 92–97.)

Howard, Kim: P.O. Box 1521, Ketchum, Idaho 83340, (208) 725-0656. Wall art, illustration, and fine art. (See fireplace, p. 147.)

Maclean, Janis: HC 57, Box 521, Reedpoint, Montana 59069, (406) 932-6537. Handmade log furniture and cabin accessories. (See Maclean house, pp. 36–41.)

Stoddard, Jim: Rocky Mountain Ivory, P.O. Box 5956, Pagosa Springs, Colorado 81147, (970) 824-6029. Hand-carved wood and antler art, furniture, and fixtures. (See Fulton house, pp. 80–85.)

Savoia-Shawback, Penny: P.O. Box 1916, Ketchum, Idaho 83340, (208) 788-4114. Interior design and Feng Shui—an ancient Chinese art involving energy flow through a home and the placement and layout of the home to optimize balance and harmony.

Triumph Metal Works, Inc.: David Harris, Box 1497, Ketchum, Idaho 83340, (208) 726-3090, Fax (208) 726-5105. Decorative and architectural metal, interior and exterior lighting, fire screens, furniture, and automatic entry gates.

Gregory Vasileff: Gregory and Liz Vasileff, 797 Pomfret Rd., Hampton, Connecticut 06247, (860) 455-9939, Fax (860) 455-9349, e-mail: gvasileff@snet.net. Specializing in convincing antique reproduction furniture. (See kitchen armoire p. 137.)

Just For Fun

1890 General Store Bed and Breakfast: Proprietors Vic and Jean Proctor, 2828 Esterbrook Rd., Douglas, Wyoming 82633, (307) 351-1765.

Buckin' Horse Bunkhouse: HC 57, Box 521, Reedpoint, Montana 59069, (406) 932-6537. Proprietors Janis and Rod Maclean accommodate the cowboy at heart in Rod's hand-built cabin that sleeps five. Continental breakfast available on request. (See p. 38.)

Organizations

American Log Builders Association: P.O. Box 28608, Bellingham, Washington 98228-0608, (360) 752-1303, Fax (360) 752-1304, e-mail: logbldassn@aol.com

and

Canadian Log Builders Association, International: 800–15355 24th Ave., Box 465, White Rock, BC, Canada V4H 2H9.

These two affiliated groups form a worldwide organization devoted to furthering the art of handcrafted log construction and to promoting the highest standards in the trade. They write and distribute educational material to builders, institutions, and industry. Call or write the Bellingham office for membership information.

Horse Logger's International Newsletter: Greg Caudell, publisher, HCO 1, Box 34-C, Keller, Washington 99140, (509) 634-4388, e-mail: gcaudell@televar.com. Dedicated to networking with those interested in the benign technology of horse logging. Also contact Greg for help locating house logs. URL: www.televar.com/~gcaudell.

Log House Builder's Association of North America, The: P.O. Box 221, Duvall, Washington 98019, (360) 794-4469, e-mail: loghouse@premier1.net, URL: //www.premier1.net/~loghouse. LHBA is an independent trade organization of handcrafters dedicated to the promulgation and preservation of the craft of log building in its truest form.

Log Homes Council: 1201 - 15th St. NW, Washington, DC 20005, (1-800) 368-5242 ext. 576, URL: www.loghomes.org. LHC members sponsor research, training, and marketing programs committed to raising industry standards. The council has developed a log home grading and certification program that all member companies must adhere to.

North American Horse and Mule Logger Association: Glen French, 8307 Salmon River Hwy, Otis, Oregon 97368, (541) 994-9765, e-mail: dfrench@efn.org. A trade association and referral service to put interested individuals in touch with professional horse loggers near them. The association also references schools and other training and educational opportunities.

Timber Products Inspection Inc.: P.O. Box 919, Conyers, Georgia 30207, (770) 922-8000, or Western Office: P.O. Box 55878, Portland, Oregon 97238, (503) 254-0204. TPI grades logs for subscribing clients as well as nonmembers. They will arrange with log home buyers to grade log packages produced by nonparticipating companies.

Building Seminars and Trade Exhibitions

Log Home Living Seminars, Inc.: 4200-T, Lafayette Center Dr., P.O. Box 220039, Chantilly, Virginia 20153, (1-800) 826-3893, URL: www.loghomeliving.com. Homebuyer Publications sponsors four major, three-day regional shows annually along with dozens of one-day, general information seminars year-round throughout the United States.

Log Building Schools

B. Allan Mackie School of Log Building in association with Daizen Log-Tech: P.O. Box 408, Coombs, BC, Canada V0R 1M0, (250) 248-0294, Fax (250) 248-6352. Month-long courses offered annually; time and dates may vary.

Great Lakes School of Log Building: Snowshoe Trail, Sand Lake, Isabella, Minnesota 55607, (218) 365-2126, e-mail: logcabin@northernnet.com, URL: www. northernnet.com/logcabin. Offers intensive, ten-day, hands-on courses year-round.

Jim Barna Log Systems Log Home Institute: P.O. Box 4529, Oneida, Tennessee 37841-4529, (1-800) 962-4734, Fax (615) 569-3792, URL: www.logcabins.com. Three-day, hands-on construction courses offered year round and free of charge to clients who purchase company-produced homes. Fees are charged to other individuals, but are refundable upon purchase of a log package. Jim Barna is the largest manufacturer of log homes in North America, producing a variety of machine-milled and hand-hewn homes.

Montana School of Log Building: Al Anderson, RR1 Box 192, Three Forks, Montana 59752, (406) 285-3488. Five-day classes in chinkless, full-round, scribed construction. Also inquire about their six-tape video package with twelve hours of building instruction.

Palmquist's The Farm: Jim and Helen Palmquist, N5136 River Road, Brantwood, Wisconsin 54513, (1-800) 519-2558. Introductory, weekend workshops in the Scandinavian chinkless style of construction offered twice annually in early spring and fall. Fees include lodging and meals at the Palmquist's cross-country ski resort.

Pat Wolfe Log Building School: 837 Richmond Rd., RR3, Ashton, ONT, Canada K0A 1B0, (613) 253-0631, Fax (613) 253-2604, URL: www.igs.net/~pwolfe, e-mail: pwolfe2istar.ca. One-, four-, or ten-week courses offered twice yearly in mid-April and mid-September. Full-scribe, round-log construction.

Skip Ellsworth's School for Log House Building: 22203 State Route 203, Monroe, Washington 98272, Tel/Fax (360) 794-4469, e-mail: loghouse@premier1.net, URL://www.premier1.net/~loghouse. Skip and his son DeWelle offer intensive weekend courses at the end of each month all year long. Logcrafters are generally available to answer building questions from the public, free of charge, at the number listed above.

Sun Country School of Log Building and Sun Country Log Works: 56206 NW Sunset Hwy, Timber, Oregon 97144, (1-800) 827-1688, Fax (503) 324-0922, e-mail: loghomes@europa.com. A variety of beginning and advanced courses offered in the spring and summer, including specialty classes tailored to meet the needs of specific groups or individuals. Purchase everything you need to build and finish your log home at the Sun Country Log Works companion resource store.

Books

IDEA DESIGN BOOKS

American Log Homes: Arthur Thiede and Cindy Teipner. Gibbs Smith, Publisher, P.O. Box 667, Layton, Utah 84041. Cindy and Art present more than 200 color and black-and-white photographs of the dozens of unique log homes they discovered in their cross-country search of America. Numerous floor plans are also included. Softcover, 192 pp., 1986.

The Log Home Book: Cindy Teipner-Thiede and Arthur Thiede. Gibbs Smith, Publisher, P.O. Box 667, Layton, Utah 84041. This bright and beautiful resource book showcases hundreds of design innovations in the log home industry. It features 200 color photographs of exteriors and interiors of classic and contemporary homes, along with a clearly illustrated section on care, maintenance, and construction. Softcover, 216 pp., 1993.

Rocky Mountain Home: Spirited Western Hideaways: Elizabeth Claire Flood. Gibbs Smith, Publisher, P.O. Box 667, Layton, Utah 84041. A romantic, photographic journey to rustic cabins and mountain hideaways in the Rocky Mountain states. Hardcover, 175 color photographs, 160 pp., 1996.

Cowboy High Style: Thomas Molesworth to the New West: Elizabeth Claire Flood. Gibbs Smith, Publisher, P.O. Box 667, Layton, Utah 84041. A beautifully photographed, readable commentary that captures the entrepreneurial and artistic spirit of Thomas Molesworth, and introduces the contemporary furniture and accessory makers who are pushing the western decorative style ahead in both craftsmanship and design. Paperback, color, 176 pp., 1992.

HOW-TO BOOKS

Alternative Housebuilding: Mike McClintock. Sterling Publishing Co., Inc., New York, New York 10016. A complete guide to constructing alternative homes that cost less to build and heat, including log, timber frame, adobe, stone, cordwood, pole, rammed-earth, and earth sheltering. Hundreds of step-by-step photos and drawings. Softcover, black-and-white, 367 pp., 1989.

Build Your Own Low-Cost Log Home: Roger Hard. Storey Communications, Inc., Schoolhouse Rd., Pownal, Vermont 05261. A basic guide for owner-builders working with their own logs or a manufacturer's kit. Includes how-to information and money-saving tips on kit selection, tools, designs, and construction. Softcover, 196 pp., revised 1985.

Build Your Dream Home for Less: R. Dodge Woodson. Betterway Books, Cincinnati, Ohio. Learn how to build a quality home and save money at every stage of construction. Teaches everything you need to know about being your own general contractor, working with materials suppliers, selecting subcontractors, getting blueprints drawn for free, financing, etc. Includes an appendix with sample forms and contracts. Softcover, 186 pp., 1995.

Building and Restoring the Hewn Log House: Charles McRaven. Betterway Books, Cincinnati, Ohio. The leading guide on building and restoring traditional hewn log houses with step-by-step instruction and advice from the nation's foremost authority on the subject. Softcover, color and black-and-white photographs and illustrations, 162 pp., second edition 1994.

Building the Timber Frame House: The Revival of a Forgotten Craft: Tedd Benson. Simon & Schuster, 200 Old Tappen Rd., Old Tappen, New Jersey 07675, (1-800) 223-2336. A comprehensive manual with step-by-step instructions on the design and construction of the timber-frame home. Softcover, heavily illustrated in black and white, 211 pp., 1981.

Building with Stone: Charles McRaven. Storey Communications, Inc., Schoolhouse Rd., Pownal, Vermont 05261. An introduction to the art and craft of creating stone structures with step-by-step instruction on building stone walls, buttresses, fireplaces, bridges, dams, homes, etc. The book also discusses restoration techniques and McRaven's philosophy of careful craftsmanship. Softcover, black-and-white photos and illustrations, 192 pp., revised edition 1989.

Code Check: Redwood Kardon. Taunton Press, P.O. Box 5506, Newtown, Connecticut 06470, (1-800) 888-8286. Gives you the correct answers to the 600 most common building code questions. Spiral bound, 36 pp., revised edition 1996.

Complete Guide to Building Log Homes: Monte Burch. Sterling Publishing Company, 387 Park Ave. S., New York, New York 10016-8810, (212) 532-7160, (1-800) 848-1186. A soup-to-nuts log homebuilding guide with more than 800 illustrations and detailed photographs. Includes land selection, site and plan development, tools, construction, insulation, information on subcontractors, etc. Softcover, 416 pp., 1990.

Do-It-Yourself Housebuilding: The Complete Handbook: George Nash. Sterling Publishing Company, 387 Park Ave. S., New York, New York 10016-8810, (1-800) 848-1186. Provides expert help in the full range of house planning and building, including specific systems like plumbing and electrical, and specific areas such as baths, kitchens, porches, and decks. With over 1,700 photos, drawings, and diagrams, this is the most complete, authoritative, and up-to-date guide ever published on housebuilding. Softcover, 704 pp., 1995.

Fine Homebuilding Great Houses: Small Houses: Taunton Press, P.O. Box 5506, Newtown, Connecticut 06470, (1-800) 888-8286. Architects and builders give you details, ideas, and options to help you build better when you build small. Softcover, color, 160 pp., 1995. Compilation of houses 2,000 square feet or less featured in *Fine Homebuilding* magazine.

Green Building Resource Guide: John Hermannsson. Taunton Press, P.O. Box 5506, Newtown, Connecticut 06470, (1-800) 888-8286. Get instant access to more than 600 environmentally responsible alternatives to common building materials. Softcover, 160 pp., 1997.

How to Fix Damn Near Anything: Franklynn Peterson. Random House, 400 Hahn Rd., Westminster, Maryland 21157, (1-800) 733-3000. An easy-to-follow guide to repairing refrigerators, air conditioners, TVs, stereo equipment, bicycles, mowers, wooden furniture, and 237 other household gadgets and appliances. Softcover, 480 pp., 1996.

Log Cabin Video: Watch the actual building of a log home, and learn how to scribe and notch logs, build an insulated roof, cut openings for windows and doors, stain and chink logs for a weather-tight seal, and rough in plumbing and electrical lines. Includes a free project guide. 140 minutes. This resource available from GCR Publishing Group, (1-800) 435-9007.

Stonework: Techniques and Projects: Charles McRaven. Storey Communications, Inc., Schoolhouse Rd., Pownal, Vermont 05261. Expert instruction on ornamental stonework and landscaping projects, including bridges, fountains, entryways, steps, and paths. Softcover, black-and-white photographs and illustrations, 183 pp., 1997.

The Natural House Book: Creating a Healthy, Harmonious, and Ecologically-Sound Home Environment: David Pearson. Simon & Schuster Inc., 200 Old Tappen Rd., Old Tappen, New Jersey 07675, (1-800) 223-2336. A comprehensive guide to designing or adapting every room in a house to be toxin-free and energy efficient for healthy, holistic living. Softcover, 100 color photos and scores of color charts and drawings, 287 pp., 1989. Also see *New Natural House Book,* softcover, 304 pp., 1998.

The Timber-Frame Home: Design, Construction, Finishing: Tedd Benson. Taunton Press, P.O. Box 5506, Newtown, Connecticut 06470, (1-800) 888-8286. Step-by-step instruction through timber-frame strategy, engineering, and design. Color, 145 photos, 130 drawings, 240 pp., revised and updated 1995.

Magazines

Bob Villa's American Home: The Hearst Corporation, 959 Eighth St., New York, New York 10019. For subscription information: P.O. Box 7476, Red Oak, Iowa 51591-0476, (1-800) 333-2784. Home repair, remodeling, styling, and restoration for the project-oriented homeowner.

Fine Homebuilding: The Taunton Press, 63 S. Main St., P.O. Box 5506, Newtown, Connecticut 06470-5506, (1-800) 283-7252, Fax (203) 270-6751. Expert instruction in all areas of general homebuilding and design with close-up photographs and detailed illustrations. Directed to the professional builder, designer, and architect.

Home Buyers Publications: 4451 Brookfield Corp. Dr., Suite 101, Chantilly, Virginia 22021, (1-800) 826-3893, Fax (703) 222-3209. Publisher of *Log Home Living* and *Timber Frame Homes* magazines. Ideas and resources for consumers who plan to build or buy log or timber-frame homes.

Homestead Communications Corp: 441 Carlisle Dr., Herndon, Virginia 22070, (703) 471-2041, Fax (703) 471-1559. Publisher of *County's Best Log Homes,* which focuses exclusively on milled log homes.

Log Home Design Ideas: H&S Media, 1620 S. Lawe St., Suite 2, Appleton, Wisconsin 54915, (1-800) 573-1900, Fax (414) 830-1710. Technical building and design information for log homebuilders and consumers.

Log Homes Illustrated Magazine: GCR Publishing Group, 1700 Broadway, 34th Floor, New York, New York 10019, (212) 541-7100, Fax (212) 245-1241. A complete consumer guide to log homes in North America.

Mother Earth News: Subscriptions: P.O. Box 56304, Boulder, Colorado 80323-6304, (303) 682-2438. An original country magazine emphasizing conservation and a self-sufficient, low-impact lifestyle.

This Old House Magazine: Time Publishing Ventures, Inc., 1185 Avenue of the Americas, New York, New York 10036, (1-800) 898-7237. New Ideas and do-it-yourself projects for old homes. Based on the popular public television series by the same name.

Traditional Building: 69A Seventh Ave., Brooklyn, New York 11217, (718) 636-0788, Fax (718) 636-0750, URL: http://www.traditionalbuilding.com/index.html#menu. A project-oriented trade publication focusing on home restoration and historically styled new construction. Editorial content is devoted to historical products: where to find them, how to evaluate them, and how to install and use them.

http://tfguild.org//index.html: This site, produced by the Timber Framers Guild, offers information on timber-frame construction and design.

http://www.woodworking.com/loghome/logassoc/index.html: This site is a good resource for anyone looking for a log builder, or for log builders looking for work. It also provides home construction information.

http://tfguild.org//index.html. This is the site of the Timber Framers Guild of North America, a nonprofit organization dedicated to promoting the benefits, beauty, and practicality of a timber-frame structure.

Web Sites

http://www.umass.edu/bmatwt/features.html: This Web site, authored by faculty and students of the wood technology department of the University of Massachusetts, contains a wealth of information regarding residential construction, including a helpful article entitled "Decoding Building Codes."

http://www.hometime.com: Based on the "Hometime" television series, this site contains information relating to log home construction.

http://www.woodworking.com/loghomes/: Another source of log home information that covers the usual topics about home construction and offers a BBS (bulletin board system) where you can communicate with others who have similar interests.